Caveman Cookbooks
PALEO GREEK RECIPES
+
PALEO GRILLING RECIPES
--
2 BOOK COMBO
By Angela Anottacelli

Caveman Cookbooks
PALEO GREEK RECIPES
By Angela Anottacelli

GREEK APPETIZERS/DIPS/SAUCES

Phyllo Dough (Filo Dough)

When it comes to Greek food, everyone needs a reliable phyllo dough (also referred to as filo dough) recipe! When you have a good phyllo recipe - the doors of Greek cooking open widely. Many Greek recipes from appetizers to man courses to snacks to desserts rely on phyllo dough sheets in their recipes. This is a simple, flaky, phyllo recipe that bakes up to puffy, golden perfection. Greek cooking in your kitchen will never again be the same!

Yield: Approximately 3-lbs. (18-20 large thin sheets)
Servings: 18-20
Total Time – Prep to Finish: 20 minutes

Ingredients:

- 8 c. of coconut or almond flour
- 2 tsp. white vinegar
- 2 tsp. extra-virgin olive oil
- juice of 1 lemon
- 1¼ - 1 1/3 c. hot water

Directions:

1. There are 2 options for rolling out these phyllo dough sheets. The first, is using the conventional rolling pin method. The second is rolling the sheets out using a pasta machine. Instructions for both methods are as follows.

2. To roll out with a rolling pin: In a large mixing bowl, add 6 c. of the flour. Make a well in the center of the flour and begin adding 1 c. of the hot water (Note: hot water is the key to this recipe's success. Get the water as hot as possible!) and the vinegar. Blend with a fork. Add in the olive oil and continue mixing, adding more hot water as needed for a soft, pliable dough that sticks together. Turn the dough out onto a floured surface and knead by hand, oiling hands if needed, for about 10 minutes or until the dough is soft, malleable, and smooth. Next, divide the dough into 18-20 equally uniform pieces and roll each piece of dough out into a rough oval-looking shape, about 18-19 inches across, sprinkling the work surface and the dough with the remaining 2 c. of flour to keep the dough from sticking. Note: the sheets of dough will be about the thickness of 2 sheets of copy paper.

3. To roll out with a pasta machine: In a large mixing bowl, combine all of the ingredients and mix by hands until it sticks together. Lay the dough out onto floured surface and continue kneading by hands for 15-20 minutes or until the dough is soft and malleable, with a smooth feel. Wrap the dough in plastic wrap and let refrigerate overnight. When the dough is ready to process through the pasta machine, consider the following: if you are creating the dough sheets for pastries, then process it through the pasta machine (settings 1-10; 1 being the thickest), gradually working the dough down to setting 9 on your machine. If you are using the phyllo sheets for recipes such as pitas, then process the dough through the machine maintaining setting #6 the entire time.

4. Use the dough right away for your recipe or store the dough by keeping it refrigerated in air-tight wrapping for up to 10 days.

Gyro Meatballs with Tzatziki Sauce

Gyro is a Greek dish that typically consists of lamb roasted on a vertical spit and then served in a sandwich or wrap with fresh veggies and Tzatziki. Tzatziki sauce is traditionally made using cucumber, yogurt, olive oil, and garlic, however, we skipped the bread and made a healthier version of the sauce with gyro-style meatballs for dipping. Healthier, yet equally delicious.

Yield: 40 meatballs
Servings: 10 (Serving Size: 4 meatballs; 2oz. sauce)
Total Time – Prep to Finish: 40 minutes

Ingredients

For the Meatballs:
- 2-lbs. fresh ground beef or lamb
- 1 c. onion, minced
- 4 cloves garlic, minced
- 6 tbsp. fresh-squeezed lemon juice
- 1 tsp. fresh lemon zest
- 2 tbsp. dried parsley
- 2 tsp. sea salt, or to taste
- 1 tsp. onion powder
- ½ tsp. Nutmeg
- 2 tsp. Cumin
- 1 tsp. dried oregano
- 1 tsp. ground black pepper, or to taste
- 2 large eggs, beaten

For the Tzatziki Sauce:
- 2 c. full-fat coconut milk (or coconut milk yogurt)
- 1½ c. cucumber, peeled & chopped fine
- 4 tbsp. fresh dill, chopped
- 2 cloves garlic, minced
- 5 tbsp. fresh-squeezed lemon juice
- Pinch of sea salt, or to taste
- Pinch of fresh ground black pepper, or to taste

Directions:

1. Preheat oven to 425°F. Spray grease a baking sheet with cooking spray.

2. Prepare the meatballs: In a large mixing bowl, combine the ground lamb (or beef), onion, minced garlic, dried parsley, sea salt, onion powder, nutmeg, cumin, dried oregano, and black pepper. Massage the spices into the meat with clean hands.

3. Next, break the eggs into a small bowl; whisk. Add the lemon juice and lemon zest to the beaten eggs; whisk. Pour the egg mixture into the bowl with the meat mixture and mix until well incorporated.

4. Roll the meat into balls using about 1 rounded tbsp. per meatball. Place them on the prepared baking sheet. Place them in the oven and bake for 10-13 minutes or until cooked through. When there is 5 minutes of baking time left, place a large skillet over medium-high heat, add the olive oil and let it heat up. When you remove the meatballs from the oven transfer them straight into the hot oil and sear them for 1-2 minutes or until they are perfectly browned on the outside. This gives the meatballs that extra crunch as if they were grilled on a spit. While the meatballs are in the oven baking, prepare the sauce with salt and black pepper, to taste.

5. Cover with plastic wrap and place in the refrigerator until ready to serve.

6. For an easy way to serve this appetizer, place toothpicks in the meatballs and divide the sauce into little 2oz. cups.

Roasted Tomatoes with Oregano & Garlic

For a traditional Greek appetizer bursting with flavor and nutrients, try these roasted tomato rounds seasoned with garlic and oregano. Besides an appetizer, this dish can also easily act as a snack or dinner side dish; or perhaps, even a light lunch when paired with bread.

Yield: about 20 (½-inch) roasted tomato rounds
Servings: 5 (Serving Size: 4 roasted tomato rounds)
Total Time – Prep to Finish: 40 minutes

Ingredients:

For the Roasted Tomatoes:
- 5 tomatoes, cut into ½-inch thick rounds
- 2 cloves of garlic, minced
- 4-6 tbsp. dried oregano
- 4-6 tbsp. breadcrumbs (see recipe)
- Salt, as needed to taste
- Black pepper, as needed to taste
- Extra-virgin olive oil, as needed

For the Breadcrumbs:
- ½ c. almond meal (or almond flour)
- ¼ c. golden flaxseed meal
- 1 tsp. garlic powder
- ½ tsp. onion powder
- ½ tsp. thyme
- ½ tsp. dried oregano
- 1¼ tsp. sea salt
- ½ tsp. fresh ground black pepper

Directions:

1. Preheat oven to 400°F.
2. Prepare the Breadcrumbs: In a medium-sized mixing bowl, combine the breadcrumb ingredients in the order listed. Mix well and use as needed. Store remaining breadcrumbs in an airtight container at room temperature for up to 2 weeks.
3. Wash and pat dry the tomatoes using paper towels. Slice the tomatoes, with the skin intact, into ½-inch rounds. Place the tomato slices on a baking sheet, using more than one baking sheet, if needed.
4. Drizzle a little olive oil over each tomato round.
5. Sprinkle the top of each tomato round with the minced garlic, dried oregano, and breadcrumbs.
6. Drizzle the tops of the tomato rounds with a little more olive oil and season each with salt

and black pepper, to taste.

7.   Place the baking sheet(s) in the preheated oven and bake for 18-20 minutes or until the tomatoes are nicely roasted and the seasoned tops are lightly golden brown. Remove from oven and let rest 5 minutes before serving.

Dolmas (Stuffed Grape Leaves)

Dolmas (Stuffed Grape Leaves) make the perfect "finger food" for parties. They are fun and flavorful treats courtesy of Mediterranean cuisine. Dolmas are typically stuffed with rice, but we are going for a grain-free twist with this yummy version involving cauliflower rice. Simple to make and so delicious, these little appetizers will go fast – try serving them with shot glasses of Tzatziki sauce for a flavor-packed duo.

Yield: 16 Dolmas (16 stuffed leaves)
Servings: 16 (Serving size: 1 Dolma)
Total Time – Prep to Finish: 1 hour 20 minutes

Ingredients:

- 2 tbsp. coconut oil
- 2/3 c. white onion, diced fine
- 2½-lbs. ground lamb or ground beef
- 2 tsp. nutmeg
- 1 tsp. cinnamon
- 1 tsp. cumin
- 2 tsp. dried oregano
- 1 tsp. dried parsley
- Sea salt, to taste
- Fresh ground black pepper, to taste
- 2 c. cauliflower, riced
- 4 tbsp. lime juice
- 16 grape leaves
- ½ c. water, divided
- 2 lemons
- 16 bay leaves

Directions:

1. Begin by preheating the oven to 350°F. Place a large skillet over medium heat; add in coconut oil and allow it to melt. Add the onion to the melted oil and sauté for 3-5 minutes or until the onion is translucent.

2. Add in the ground meat, nutmeg, cinnamon, cumin, oregano, parsley, and salt/black pepper, to taste. Stir well to incorporate, then cook for 5-7 minutes or until only a small amount of pink remains. Add more salt and pepper as needed to taste.

3. Rice the cauliflower by grating the florets with a cheese grater or by pulsing a few times with a food processor and then stir it in to the meat mixture. Cook for 2-3 minutes. Stir in the lime juice. Remove from heat.

4. Place two (9 x 13-inch) baking dishes next to the grape leaves on a flat work surface. Gently separate the grape leaves and lay them out one by one. Spoon 1-2 tbsp. of the meat mixture onto the center of each grape leaf towards the stem. Roll the bottom of the leaf up and over the mixture, fold in the sides, and continue to roll until the tip of the leaf is tucked underneath.

5. Slice the other halves of the lemons thinly. Top each dolma with bay leaves and place a

thin slice of lemon on top of each dolma.

6. Cover the baking dishes with aluminum foil, place the baking dishes in the preheated oven and bake for 30-35 minutes or until the water has almost entirely evaporated.

7. Remove the bay leaves before serving. Dolmas are good served hot or cold. Serve with Tzatziki sauce, if desired.

Melitzanosalata (Eggplant Dip)

This classic Greek eggplants dip is often served with appetizers and salads. The basic dip is prepared by combining eggplant, olive oil, garlic, and wine vinegar. Other versions often incorporate tomato as well. This is a very simple, very quick dip to prepare and is a hit at parties.

Yield: 3 cups dip
Servings: 12 (Serving size: ¼ cup)
Total Time – Prep to Finish: 10 minutes

Ingredients:

- 2 large eggplants
- 1 c. extra-virgin olive oil
- 8 tsp. wine vinegar
- 6 cloves garlic
- Sea salt, to taste
- Fresh ground black pepper, to taste

Directions:

1. Preheat the grill to medium-high heat. Using a fork, piece a few holes in the eggplants then char them over the hot grill for about 5 minutes or until the eggplants turn black and are very soft. Place paper towels under a wire rack, then set the eggplants on the wire rack to cool and drain. When the eggplants are cool enough to handle, peel them by hand and transfer the peeled eggplants to a large bowl. Chop the eggplant pulp into very small pieces, then mash with a fork.

2. Using a wooden spoon, gradually stir in the olive oil and wine vinegar, alternating between the oil and the vinegar. Stir until the dip is smooth, but chunky.

3. Stir in the minced garlic and then season the dip with sea salt and black pepper, to taste. Serve the dip chilled or at room temperature.

Avga Gemista (Greek Stuffed Eggs)

Avga Gemista is a Greek finger food often served as appetizers. It involves mixing the yolk with ground beets and spooning the mixture into the hard-boiled egg white shells, in the same manner you would if you were making deviled eggs. This is a quick appetizer or snack that is nutritious and delicious!

Yield: 12 stuffed eggs
Servings: 12 (Serving size: 1 stuffed egg)
Total Time – Prep to Finish: 10 minutes

Ingredients:

- 12 hard-boiled eggs, shelled
- 1/2 cup minced cooked beet
- 4 teaspoons minced capers
- 3 tablespoons snipped fresh parsley
- 2 tablespoons lemon juice
- 1/4 cup mayonnaise
- salt and pepper
- 1 whole capers

Directions:

1. Hard-boil the eggs, then let cool. Remove the shells and cut the eggs in half crosswise. Remove the yolks and place in a bowl. Cut a very thin slice from the bottom of each egg so that the eggs can stand upright on their own.

2. Cook the beets and then ground the beets to yield ½ c. Add the cooked ground beets, minced cpers, snipped parsley, lemon juice, and salt/black pepper, to taste into the bowl with the egg yolks. Using a food processor, immersion blender, or electric hand mixer, beat the yolk mixture until smooth.

3. Spoon the mixture into the egg white shells and form a small mound on the top of each egg white shell. Decorate each egg with a caper and serve.

Kritisinia - Greek Breadsticks with Carrot & Parsley

In Greece, breadsticks are referred to as "Kritisinia" and they, along with many other types of bread, are a major part of most meals. Historically, in villages throughout Greece, when times were economically tough, bread was a crucial staple in the Greek diet because it filled the villagers up quickly and kept them full until they were able to eat again. Since then, the tradition of having some type of bread during meals has lived on in the homes of the Greek people. This recipe is a popular version of kritisinia ; having carrots and parsley rolled up right in the dough, it makes for a flavorful and more nutritious bread.

Yield: about 12 breadsticks
Servings: 6 (Serving size: 2 breadsticks)
Total Time – Prep to Finish: 55 minutes

Ingredients:

- 2 c. almond flour (or coconut flour)
- 3 tsp. baking powder
- ½ tsp. salt
- ½ c. extra-virgin olive oil
- ½ c. water
- 1 tsp. vinegar
- 1 tsp. coconut palm sugar
- 4½ oz. carrots, shredded
- 2-3 tbsp. fresh parsley, chopped

Directions:

1. Preheat the oven to 350°F. Line a baking sheet with parchment paper.

2. In a large mixing bowl, combine the flour, baking powder, and salt. Sift well to blend.

3. In a small bowl, combine the water, vinegar, and coconut palm sugar. Whisk until the sugar is mostly dissolved.

4. Gradually add in the olive oil and the vinegar-water mixture to the flour mixture and mix with a dough hook for 2-3 minutes (or clean hands) until a nice dough forms.

5. Fold the carrots and parsley into the dough and mix with a wooden spoon or by hand.

6. On a floured surface, roll the dough out into thin bread sticks. Place each breadstick onto the parchment-lined baking sheet.

7. Place the baking sheet into the preheated oven and bake for 25-30 minutes or until the breadsticks are lightly browned and no longer doughy. Keep a watchful eye on the breadsticks during baking to ensure that they do not over bake. Remove the breadsticks from the oven and let cool for 5-10 minutes before serving.

Pseftokeftedes Santorini - Greek Veggie Patties

Pseftokeftedes Santorini is a Greek-styled veggie burger. Different types of patties made from a large variety of vegetables, legumes, and other non-meat ingredients are very much a part of the Mediterranean diet – from bean patties, to falafels, to tomato patties, to zucchini fritters known as "kolokithoketedes," and everything in between, the Greeks have traditionally been known to cherish their vegetables – particularly in patty form. Throughout Greece, non-meat patties are often referred to as "pseftokeftedes" or "pseudo-patties" because they do not contain any type of meat and are not considered "real" patties – however, these "pseudo-patties" are frequently seen on dinner tables, at parties, and at restaurants throughout Greece. They are considered delicious and healthy and every bit worth the lack of meat!

Yield: about 36 patties
Servings: 36 (Serving size: 1 patty)
Total Time – Prep to Finish: 1 hour

Ingredients:

- 1-2 large ripe plum tomato(es), peeled and chopped (yield 1¼ c. chopped tomato)
- ½ c. scallions, chopped fine
- 1 clove garlic, chopped fine
- 1 tbsp. fresh parsley, chopped
- 1 heaping tsp. fresh mint chopped
- ½ tsp. dried oregano
- ¼ tsp. ground cinnamon
- Pinch of salt, as needed to taste
- Pinch of fresh ground black pepper, as needed to taste
- 1 c. coconut flour (or almond flour or arrowroot flour)
- 1 tsp. double-acting baking powder
- Extra-virgin olive oil, as needed for frying

Directions:

1. In a large mixing bowl, combine the tomatoes, scallions, garlic, herbs, and spices. Stir to blend well.

2. Stir in the flour and baking powder; mix until very well incorporated and form a batter similar to pancake batter.

3. Place a large, heavy-bottomed skillet over medium heat, Add in just enough olive oil to barely fill the bottom of the skillet (you only want the bottom of the patties to be touching the oil; you do not want there to be oil coming up the sides of the patties); let the oil heat up.

4. When the oil is hot, take a heaping tbsp. of the batter and drop it right into the middle of the hot oil. Fry as many patties as you can at once without them touching one another. Fry each patty for 2-4 minutes or until the patties are perfectly crisp and golden browned. As soon as the patties become cooked, remove them immediately with a slotted spatula or slotted spoon and lay them on paper towels to rid themselves of any excess grease. Serve hot.

Marinated Greek Olives

Marinated Greek olives are often gifted during the holidays throughout Greece. They make a great gift for friends, neighbors, co-workers, etc. because they taste great and are jarred to maintain a long shelf life. This recipe includes the recipes for two types of marinated Greek olives. However, for the second recipe, the Moroccan Spiced Olives, that can act as a two-part recipe with the Marinated Greek Olives or you can use plain black olives. You are able to make one or both types of marinated olives – whenever you are in the need for some marinated Greek olives, here are two tasty recipes to follow!

Yield: 4 c. olives PER recipe
Servings: 32 (Serving size: ¼ c. olives)
Total Time – Prep to Finish: 2 hours 5 minutes

Ingredients:

For the Marinated Greek Olives (Elies Marinates):

- 4 c. black and/or green olives
- ¾ c. extra-virgin olive oil
- ½ c. red wine vinegar (or lemon juice)
- 1 tsp. dried oregano, crushed
- 1 leek, white part only, slices
- 2 orange slices
- 1 lemon, sliced
- 1 bay leaf

For the Moroccan Spiced Olives (Meslalla):

- 1 c. Marinated Greek Olives (or plain black olives)
- 3 tbsp. lemon juice
- 1 tsp. paprika
- ½ tsp. ground cumin
- 1 garlic clove, minced
- 1 tbsp. extra-virgin olive oil
- 2 tbsp. fresh parsley, chopped
- Sea salt, to taste
- Fresh ground black pepper, to taste

Directions:

1. Prepare the Marinated Greek Olives (Elies Marinates): Combine all ingredients in a mixing bowl. Mix well. Cover the bowl with plastic wrap and marinate in the refrigerator for at least 2 hours.

2. Prepare the Moroccan Spiced Olives (Meslalla): Combine all ingredients in a medium-sized mixing bowl. Mix well. Cover the bowl with plastic wrap and marinate in the refrigerator for at least 2 hours.

3. Pour the marinated olives into separate jars with tight-fitting lids. Then store or serve and enjoy!

Baked Eggplant Rounds

In Greek cooking, eggplant is one of the most widely used foods. It is grilled, baked, stewed, fried, pulped, and more. It is served at most parties and celebrations as appetizers, snacks, and main courses and at home, it can be eaten at any meal, and sometimes when abundant, it may even be eaten at more than one meal per day! Look in any Greek cookbook and you will find that eggplant is listed as an ingredient multiple times. For this simple to prepare and delicious appetizer (or snack - or even side dish) we are baking eggplant rounds and topping them with tomato sauce and crumbled feta – the flavors meld together heavenly!

Yield: about 28 baked eggplant rounds
Servings: 14 (Serving Size: 2 baked eggplant rounds)
Total Time – Prep to Finish: 20 minutes

Ingredients:

- 3-4 large eggplants, cut into ½-inch thick rounds
- 3 tbsp. plus 28 tsp. extra-virgin olive oil, divided
- 1-2 white onion(s), chopped fine
- 4-6 large, ripe tomatoes, chopped (or 2 cans chopped tomatoes)
- Salt, to season, as needed
- Fresh ground black pepper, to season, as needed
- 1 tsp. coconut palm sugar
- 2 c. Daiya feta cheese, crumbled, to garnish
- Fresh parsley, chopped fine, to garnish

Directions:

1. Wash each eggplant and pat dry with paper towel. Leaving the skin intact, slice each eggplant into ½-inch thick slices. Place the sliced eggplant in a colander and salt to season, then let sit at room temperature for 60 minutes.

2. Preheat the oven to 350°F. Place a large skillet over medium heat, add 1 tbsp. olive oil and let it heat up. When the oil is hot, add the onion and sauté for 3-4 minutes or until translucent. Add in the tomato, a pinch each of salt and black pepper, and 1 tsp. coconut palm sugar. Stir to combine, then reduce heat to medium-low and let simmer, stirring often, for 20 minutes.

3. Once the eggplant has sat out for 1 hour, rinse the eggplant slices under cool running water and then use paper towels to gently squeeze out any excess water. In a separate skillet, over medium heat, add in 2 tbsp. olive oil and let it heat up. When the oil is hot, add in the sliced eggplant and sauté lightly for about 5 minutes, then lay out the sliced eggplant on paper towel, covering both sides with the paper towel.

4. Spray grease 1 or 2 baking sheets (with rimmed sides) with cooking spray. Arrange the eggplant rounds in a single layer; use more than one baking sheet if need be. Spoon the tomato sauce on to the top of each eggplant round, covering the surface of each sliced round very well. Drizzle each slice with 1 tsp. olive oil and then add 1-2 tsp. of crumbled feta on top of each eggplant round.

5. Place the eggplant rounds in the preheated oven and bake for 20-25 minutes or until the

eggplant is lightly browned and tender crisp. Remove from oven. Before serving, sprinkle a pinch of fresh chopped parsley over the top of each baked round, to garnish, if desired.

GREEK BREAKFASTS

Greek Spanakopita

This spinach quiche is a classic Greek spinach "pie" dish, referred to as Spanakopita. It consists of a flaky, golden pastry crust which is then loaded with Greek feta cheese and fresh chopped spinach. This dish is perfect for a filling breakfast or brunch, but can also be an excellent choice for lunch and dinner as well!

Yield: 1 (9-inch) quiche
Servings: 3-4 (Serving Size: (2) small-medium-size wedges)
Total Time – Prep to Finish: 50 minutes

Ingredients:

For the Quiche Filling:

- 3 large eggs
- 1 c. full-fat coconut milk
- ¼ c. coconut oil, melted
- 2 tbsp. coconut flour
- ¼ tsp. Celtic sea salt, or to taste
- ¼ tsp. fresh ground black pepper, or to taste
- 3 tbsp. Dayia vegan Romano cheese, grated
- Pinch of nutmeg
- 1-lb. frozen chopped spinach, Thawed & drained
- 1 c. Dayia vegan Feta cheese, crumbled

For the Quiche Pastry Crust:

- 2 c. blanched almond flour
- ¼ tsp. Celtic sea salt
- 2 tbsp. coconut oil
- 1 large egg

Directions:

1. Preheat oven to 350°F. Grease two 9" baking pans and line with parchment circles.

2. Prepare pastry crust: In a food processor, combine the almond flour and salt. Pulse to blend. Add in the egg and coconut oil and pulse again until the mixture forms a ball of pliable dough. Press the dough into a 9-inch pie dish. Poke several holes across the sides and bottom of the dough and then place it in the preheated oven and let bake for 7-10 minutes or until lightly golden.

3. Prepare the spinach-feta filling: In a large mixing bowl, whisk together the eggs. Then swhisk in the coconut milk, coconut oil, coconut flour, salt, and black pepper, Romano cheese, and nutmeg. Blend well.

4. Next, stir in the spinach and feta cheese. When well incorporated, pour the spinach-feta filling into the baked pastry shell. Smooth out the top of the quiche.

5. Place the quiche in the oven and bake for 30-35 minutes or until the eggs are set and the

center is firm, yet springy to the touch. Remove from oven, let sit 5 minutes, then slice and serve.

Greek Frittata

Frittatas are perfect for breakfast, brunch, lunch or even dinner. Frittatas are also often turned into appetizers and desserts. This recipe is for a Greek-inspired frittata which is certain to be a hit around the dining room table. For a fun twist that the kiddos will love, divide the frittata mixture between ramekins and bake for individual-sized frittatas!

Yield: 1 10-inch frittata
Servings: 4 (Serving Size: 2 wedges of frittata)
Total Time – Prep to Finish: 40 minutes

Ingredients:

- 3 tbsp. extra-virgin olive oil
- 10 large eggs
- 2 tsp. kosher salt
- ½ tsp. fresh ground black pepper
- 1 c. baby spinach, chopped or torn
- 1 pint grape tomatoes, halved
- 4 scallions - white and green parts, sliced thin
- 1 c. Daiya vegan Feta cheese, crumbled

Directions:

1. Preheat oven to 350°F.

2. Pour the olive oil into a round casserole dish and place in the preheated oven for 5 minutes.

3. While the oil is in the oven, in a large mixing bowl, combine the eggs, salt, and black pepper. Whisk to beat the eggs. Stir in the spinach, tomato, and scallion, Stir to incorporate. Then gently stir in the crumbled Daiya feta cheese.

4. Remove the hot casserole dish from the oven and pour the frittata egg mixture into the casserole dish. Place the dish back into the oven and bake for 25-30 minutes or until the edges are slightly browned and the eggs are set and slightly puffed. Remove the frittata from the oven. Slice into wedges and serve hot.

Tiganites

These airy, crispy, miniature pancake-like treats are perfect for breakfast and brunch, but are also often served as appetizers, snacks, lunch, and more. Traditionally, in many Greek villages, tiganites are prepared with only flour and water to make a runny, yet thick batter that could be fried. After, villagers would drizzle on honey and cinnamon. Many people still make tiganites that same way today, however, since those days, more ingredients have been added to the preparation. How you choose to make tiganites is a personal preference, but here is a sweet and perfectly crispy recipe to get you started!

Yield: 12-16 tiganites
Servings: 4 (Serving Size: 3-4 tiganites)
Total Time – Prep to Finish: minutes

Ingredients:

- 2 c. coconut flour (or almond flour)
- 2 c. coconut milk (or almond milk)
- 2 large eggs
- 2 tbsp. extra-virgin olive oil
- 2 tsp. arrowroot powder (opt.)
- 1 tsp. salt
- Olive oil, for frying (or coconut oil, if preferred)
- Honey for topping
- Ground cinnamon (or coconut palm sugar), to garnish
- 1 c. walnuts, chopped, to garnish (opt.)

Directions:

1. In a large mixing bowl, sift together the coconut flour (or almond flour) with the arrowroot powder (optional, but recommended as it makes the tiganites fluffier) and the salt.

2. In a separate smaller bowl, crack and beat the eggs, and then stir in the olive oil and coconut milk (or almond milk); blend well. Pour the egg mixture in with the flour mixture. Blend until well incorporated and a smooth batter forms. Add a litter more milk, if you prefer thinner pancakes.

3. Place a skillet over medium-high heat. Add a tbsp. of olive oil (or coconut oil, if preferred) and allow it to heat up. Once the olive oil is heated, drop a dollop of the batter into the center of the skillet, the batter will spread out into the shape of a disc as it cooks. Cook for about 2 minutes or until the edges of the tiganite begins to dry and bubbles appear, flip the pancake to cook the other side for approximately 2 more minutes or until crisp and golden. Remove from pan and repeat using the remaining batter to make the rest of the tiganites. If your skillet is large enough you can cook more than one tiganite at a time, or have a skillet going on each burner to prepare the tiganites more quickly.

4. To serve, place 3 to 4 tiganites on each plate. Drizzle the tiganites with honey and sprinkle on a little cinnamon or coconut palm sugar. You may also add some chopped walnuts, if desired. Serve hot.

24

Spinach & Feta Quiche

For an impressive looking Greek breakfast, prepare this delicious spinach and feta quiche. This is a versatile breakfast that is incredibly simple to personalize with different ingredients. This quiche is also an excellent choice for a quick and different dinnertime recipe.

Yield: 1 quiche
Servings: 4 (Serving Size: 1 wedge)
Total Time – Prep to Finish: 35 minutes
Ingredients:

- 1 c. frozen spinach, thawed and drained
- 8 large eggs
- ¼ c. almond milk (or preferred non-dairy milk)
- ½ c. Daiya Feta cheese, crumbled

Directions:

1. Preheat oven to 350°F. Grease a round baking pan/dish (such as a pie plate) with cooking spray.

2. Arrange the thawed spinach out across the bottom of the baking pan.

3. In a separate bowl, crack and beat the eggs and then whisk in the almond milk. Pour the egg mixture into the baking dish over top of the spinach.

4. Sprinkle the crumbled feta over the egg mixture and then stir to blend the ingredients together.

5. Place the baking dish in the preheated oven and bake for 25-30 minutes or until eggs are set and the quiche is lightly browned around the edges. Remove from oven and let sit for 5 minutes, then slice into 4 wedges and place 1 wedge on each serving dish and serve.

Portokalia me Meli (Orange with Honey)

In addition to being a popular dessert throughout Greece, Portokalia me Meli (Orange with Honey) is also an excellent option for breakfast. It is sweet, fruity, and makes the perfect start to any day. This is a simple, quick dessert that is as easy as 1-2-3!

Yield: 2 Oranges with Honey
Servings: 4 (Serving Size: 1 orange with honey)
Total Time – Prep to Finish: 5 minutes

Ingredients:

- 2 oranges, sliced into rounds, then peels removed and discarded
- Greek thyme honey (or preferred honey), to taste
- ground cinnamon, to taste (opt,)

Directions:

1. Prepare orange by slicing each into rounds that are approximately ¼-inch thick, Remove and discard the peels only after the oranges have been sliced into rounds as the peels will help to give you better control over cutting the slices.

2. Arrange the orange slices on each plate, then drizzle honey over the slices and sprinkle with ground cinnamon, if desired. Then serve and enjoy!

GREEK LUNCHES

Greek Pie

Pies aren't just for dessert! This pie brings together the bold, tangy, and unforgettable flavor combination of Kalamata olives, mint, and citrus – like a perfect salad on golden, flaky crust. This will instantly become a lunchtime favorite!

Yield: 1 (8-inch) pie
Servings: 6-8 (Serving Size: 1 slice of pie)
Total Time – Prep to Finish: 40 minutes

Ingredients:

For the crust:
- c. almond flour
- 1/3 c. extra-virgin olive oil
- Zest of ½ orange
- 1 large egg

For the filling:
- 2 tbsp. extra-virgin olive oil
- ½ red onion (or white onion, if preferred)
- 1 c, Kalamata olives, pitted and halved
- Zest of ½ lemon
- 1 tsp. sesame seeds
- 1 tbsp. fresh mint leaves, shredded

Directions:

1. Preheat oven to 350°F. Spray grease an 8-inch tart/pie pan; set aside.

2. Prepare the crust: Combine the almond flour, olive oil, orange zest, and egg into a large mixing bowl. Stir until well incorporated and pliable dough forms. Press the dough into the tart pan, thinly and evenly, so that it covers the base and sides. Using a fork, press a few holes in the bottom of the dough and place in preheated oven. Bake for about 15 minutes. The surface of the crust should be foamy and oily when you take it out of the oven, but will dry as it cools.

3. Prepare the filling: To make the filling, heat the 2 tbsp. olive oil in a medium skillet over medium heat. Add in the onion and sauté 3-5 minutes or until very tender. Remove from the heat; let onion cool, then add in the Kalamata olives and blend. Transfer the mixture to the cooled crust.

4. To finish, grate the lemon zest over the surface of the pie, then garnish by sprinkling the pie with sesame seeds and the fresh mint. Serve cold or at room temperature.

Tonosalata (Greek Tuna Salad)

For a cool, crisp, refreshingly satisfying meal on a hot spring or summer day, take a bight out of this tuna salad made using flaky tuna, crunchy celery, a creamy homemade mayonnaise, a hint of citrus, and capers. Serve over a bed of salad greens to really tie the salad together

Yield: 4 cups salad
Servings: 4 (Serving Size: 1 ¼ c. salad; 2 large bibb leaves)
Total Time – Prep to Finish: 40 minutes

Ingredients:

- 2 (6oz.) cans chunk-light tuna (packed in water), drained
- ½ c. celery, chopped fine
- 6 tbsp. paleo-friendly mayonnaise
- 4 tsp. lemon juice
- 4 tbsp. capers
- ½ tsp. lemon zest
- 8 large Bibb lettuce leaves

Directions:

1. Combine the tuna, celery, mayonnaise, and lemon juice into a small mixing bowl. Mix gently to combine.
2. Stir in ¼ tsp. of the lemon zest and 2 tbsp. of the capers. Mix well.
3. Lay out 1-2 large Bibb leaves on each plate and scoop approximately 1¼ c. of the tuna salad onto the bed of Bibb lettuce. Serve immediately. Store any remaining tuna salad in the refrigerator, covered tightly with plastic wrap.

Avgolemono (Egg-Lemon)

Avgolemono (or "Egg-Lemon") is a variety of Mediterranean-based soups and sauces that are made by combining lemon juice and eggs mixed with a broth which is then heated until it thickens. Meats, vegetables, rices, etc. are then added to the soup. Avgolemono can be served as a thick stew, a thin broth, and any consistency in between.

Yield: 12 cups soup
Servings: 8 (Serving Size: 1½ cups soup)
Total Time – Prep to Finish: 40 minutes

Ingredients:

- 4 c. chicken, fully-cooked and shredded
- 10 c. chicken broth (or chicken stock, if preferred)
- 3 eggs
- 1/3 c. fresh-squeezed lemon juice (3-4 large lemons)
- 2 c. spaghetti squash, cooked
- Sea salt, to taste
- Fresh ground black pepper, to taste
- ¼ c. fresh parsley, chopped, to garnish (opt.)
- Daiya parmesan cheese, grated, to garnish (opt.)

Directions:

1. Boil the chicken until cooked through and then shred the chicken, if not already done.

2. Cook the spaghetti squash until tender and spaghetti "noodles" part easily.

3. Place a Dutch oven or large saucepan over medium-high heat and add in the shredded chicken and chicken broth; bring contents to a boil. Remove from the heat.

4. In a medium-sized mixing bowl, whisk together the eggs and lemon juice until frothy. Gradually whisk 2 c. of the hot broth into the egg mixture. Once the broth is incorporated, add the mixture back into the Dutch oven.

5. Stir in the spaghetti squash and gently reheat the soup over medium-low heat, if necessary, but be careful to not let the contents come to a boil or the eggs may curdle. Season the soup with salt and pepper, to taste, then ladle into serving bowls. Garnish with fresh parsley and Daiya grated parmesan cheese, if desired, the serve hot and enjoy!

Tomato & Caper Salad

For a light, satisfying Mediterranean lunch, try out this salad combining ripe, plump, and juicy red tomatoes and sun-dried capers, which are drizzled with and tossed in olive oil and sprinkled with dried oregano. This is a simple Greek salad which can be prepared in as little as 5 minutes and can be served at room temperature or chilled. For an authentic Greek lunch, use Santorini capers and pair the salad with bread. This salad also serves as an excellent side dish for dinner or as a pre-dinner salad.

Yield: 4 salads
Servings: 4 (Serving Size: 2 sliced tomatoes; 1-2 tsp. capers, olive oil)
Total Time – Prep to Finish: 40 minutes

Ingredients:

- 8 ripe, red tomatoes, sliced into ¼-inch thick rounds
- 8 tsp. capers, rinsed
- Pinch of oregano, to garnish
- Extra-virgin olive oil, as needed for dressing

Directions:

1. Wash the tomatoes, pat dry with paper towel.

2. Leaving the skin of the tomatoes intact, slice 2 of the tomatoes into ¼-inch thick rounds.

3. Arrange the sliced tomato rounds on a salad plate. Drizzle on a few drops of olive, sprinkle the tomatoes with a pinch of dried oregano, and then, sprinkle on the capers.

4. Repeat to prepare the remaining 3 salads.

5. Serve at room temperature or chilled.

Lahanodolmades (Stuffed Cabbage Leaves)

Lahanodolmades, (or stuffed cabbage) are a Greek tradition of stuffing cabbage rolls with meats and rices. The stuffed cabbages leaves are then traditionally drizzled in an Avgolemono (Egg-Lemon) sauce. It is a very popular dish in many locations throughout Greece - Lahanodolmades is to Greece what Macaroni and Cheese is to America – a classic, comfort food for people of all ages!

Yield: 8 stuffed cabbage leaves
Servings: 4 (Serving Size: 2 stuffed cabbage leaves)
Total Time – Prep to Finish: 40 minutes

Ingredients:

For the Stuffed Cabbage Leaves:

- 1-lb. ground beef
- 2 c. cauliflower, riced
- 8 large cabbage leaves
- 2 red onion(s), chopped
- 2 tbsp. parsley, chopped
- 4 garlic cloves, minced
- 2 tbsp. extra-virgin olive oil
- 2 c. bone marrow broth
- 1½ c. Water
- 1-lb. ground beef

For the Avgolemono Sauce:

- 2 large eggs, room temperature (whites/yolks separated)
- 2 large lemons
- sea salt, to taste
- fresh ground black pepper, to taste

Directions:

1. Gently wash the cabbage leaves and pat dry with a paper towel, being careful to not tear the leaves. Fill a large pot of water ¾ of the way full with water and bring the water to a boil. Add the leaves to the water and make sure they are completely immersed. Let the leaves sit, immersed, in the boiling water for about 4-5 minutes or just until they begin to wilt – but not cook. Remove the leaves from the water and discard the water. Set the wilted cabbage leaves aside until needed.

2. Place a skillet over medium heat and cook the ground beef for 5-7 minutes or until browned. Remove from heat. Meanwhile, using a cheese grater, "rice" the cauliflower and set it aside.

3. In a large mixing bowl, combine the cooked ground beef, "riced" cauliflower, chopped onion, minced garlic, and fresh parsley. Using clean hands, mix the meat mixture until well blended. Generously season with sea salt and black pepper, to taste.

4. Layout the cabbage leaves onto a flat work surface. Add about 1/8 c. (give or take) of the meat mixture to the lower, thicker part of each cabbage leaf. Roll each cabbage leaf once, pause to fold the sides inwards, then continue rolling until all leaves are stuffed.

5. Pack the stuffed cabbage leaves, seam side down, into the bottom of a cooking pot. The tighter they are packed into the bottom of the pot, the better they will keep rolled and intact. You want the stuffed cabbage to be side by side touching with as little room to move about as possible. If you have completed the first layer of stuffed cabbage leaves and still have some remaining, then you can begin a second layer by laying the stuffed cabbage directly over the first layer, covering any gaps.

6. Add into the pot, with the stuffed leaves, the bone marrow broth, olive oil, and 1½ c. water just until the cabbage is immersed in the liquid.

7. Cook over medium heat for 30-40 minutes or until the liquid has evaporated just enough for the stuffed cabbage to no longer be immersed. Remove pot from the heat.

8. Prepare the Avgolemono sauce: In a deep plate, place the egg white (reserve the yolk in a small bowl until needed), Beat the egg white with a whisk for 3-4 minutes or until the egg white is frothy and creamy. Add in the yolk and beat for 1 minute. Add the lemon juice; beat for 30 seconds.

9. Using a ladle, carefully remove some of the broth (make sure that the broth is not too hot or the egg will cook) and gradually whisk it into the egg-lemon mixture. Keep adding and beating the broth, until the mixture is frothy, then pour the contents of the deep plate into the pot with the cabbage leaves and then gently tilt the pot in all directions. The Avgolemono sauce should now be thick.

10. Divide the stuffed cabbage leaves among serving plates (2 stuffed cabbage leaves per serving) and then spoon the The Avgolemono sauce over the stuffed cabbage. Sprinkle a bit of black pepper (and sea salt, if needed) over the cabbage rolls. Then serve and enjoy!

Horta Vrasta (Boiled Leafy Greens)

Horta Vrasta is a common staple in the traditional Greek diet. The leafy greens often chosen for this dish are often gathered in the wild, then washed well and boiled. The greens used can be sweet, bitter, mild-tasting or flavorful – the types of greens used often change in order to keep things interesting. For this recipe, we are using Curly Endive, which is an excellent type of leafy green to use for this dish.

Yield: 8 cups Horta Vrasta
Servings: 4 (Serving Size: 2 cups Horta Vrasta)
Total Time – Prep to Finish: 35 minutes

Ingredients:

- 3-lbs. curly Endive
- White vinegar, for soaking water
- 1 tbsp. sea salt
- 2 tbsp. extra-virgin olive oil, plus more as needed
- Juice of 1 lemon
- Sea salt, to taste
- Fresh ground black pepper, to taste

Directions:

1. First, wash the curly endive well; cut away any tough stems and throw out any brown leaves.

2. Soak the greens in a clean sink filled with water and about 1 c. of white vinegar to remove any residue, dirt, or sand stuck to the greens.

3. Transfer the greens to a colander; drain the water.

4. Place a large pot of water over high heat. Add in 1 tbsp. salt and bring the water to a boil. Place the greens in the boiling water so that they are immersed in the water and let the greens boil got about 18-20 minutes or until the thickest part of the stems become tender. Do not allow the greens to over boil.

5. Drain the greens in a colander and place them in a large bowl. Drizzle the greens with more olive oil and the lemon juice, then toss to coat well. Season with salt and black pepper, to taste. Serve immediately.

Horiatiki Salata (Country Salad)

There are many variations to a classic Greek salad. In Greece, salad is a vital component to the traditional diet This version is known as Horiatiki Salata or Greek Country Salad. Simple and fast, you can have an authentic Greek salad in front of you in mere minutes. You may be surprised to find that this recipe calls for no lettuce whatsoever!

Yield: 4 salads
Servings: 4 (Serving Size: 1 salad)
Total Time – Prep to Finish: 15 minutes

Ingredients:

- 4-5 large, ripe red tomatoes
- 1 large red onion
- 1 cucumber
- 1 green bell pepper
- ¼-lb. Daiya Feta cheese, crumbled
- Pinch dried oregano
- Sea salt, to taste
- Extra-virgin olive oil
- 12 large Kalamata olives
- Pickled pepperoncini peppers, to garnish
- 4 tbsp. water, divided (opt.)

Directions:

1. First, wash the vegetables and pat dry with paper towel. Remove the outer skin from the onion; wash and dry as well.

2. Cut the tomatoes, remove the cores, and slice into bite-size pieces. Then lightly season with sea salt.

3. Slice the cucumber in ¼ -inch slices, you can keep the peel intact, if desired. Slice the rounds in half. Lightly season the cucumber with sea salt.

4. Slice the bell pepper into thin rings, removing the stem and seeds. Lightly season with sea salt.

5. Slice the onion into thin rounds.

6. Combine the cut vegetables into a large salad bowl. Sprinkle with dried oregano. Drizzle olive oil over the salad; toss to coat.

7. Divide the salad among 4 salad plates. Top with crumbled feta cheese and sprinkle the cheese with dried oregano and black pepper, if desired. Add a few olives to each salad. Mix some more olive oil with 1 tbsp. water and drizzle over the top of one of the salads. Repeat wth the remaining 3 tbsp. of water for each salad. Garnish with pepperoncini peppers and serve.

GREEK DINNERS

Melitzanes Papoutsakia (Little Shoes)

Melitzanes Papoutsakia is Greek for "Little Shoes." A fitting description for this traditional Greek dish as the eggplant halves resemble little shoes when they are served. Melitzanes Papoutsakia are typically stuffed full of a ground beef mixture, cheese, and then drizzled with a creamy béchamel sauce.

Yield: 8 stuffed eggplant halves
Servings: 8 (Serving Size: half an eggplant with filling)
Total Time – Prep to Finish: 45 minutes

Ingredients:

For the Stuffed Eggplants:
- 2-3 tbsp. grass-fed butter (or ghee)
- 1 medium white onion, chopped
- 1-lb. ground beef
- 2-3 tbsp. plus 1/8 -1/4 c. Water
- ½ c. red wine vinegar
- 1 can tomatoes (include juices) or use 1 can paste
- ½ bunch fresh parsley, chopped
- ½ tsp. sea salt, or to taste
- ¼ tsp. fresh ground black pepper, or to taste
- 4 large, long, ripe eggplants
- Extra-virgin olive oil (for frying)
- 8 more tbsp. Dayia Vegan cheddar cheese, shredded – to garnish

For the Béchamel Sauce:
- 2-3 tbsp. grass-fed butter (or ghee)
- 5 tbsp. coconut flourv
- 11/3 c. hot full-fat coconut milk
- Pinch of salt, or to taste
- 8 tbsp. Dayia cheddar, shredded
- 2 large eggs

Directions:

1. Place a large skillet over medium heat. Add in butter and let melt, then immediately add in the chopped onion. Sauté for about 3 minutes or until the onion is translucent and fork tender.

2. Add in the ground beef along with 2-3 tbsp. water. As you cook, break the beef up with a spatula, and continue cooking for 5- 7 minutes or until browned through.

3. Add in the wine, tomatoes (and the tomato juices), parsley, and season to taste with salt and pepper. Add in the 1/8 c. water, more if needed, and then reduce heat to medium-low and let contents simmer for about 10 minutes or until all of the liquid has evaporated.

Remove skillet from heat.

4. Prepare the eggplant by rinsing in cold water, patting them dry with paper towels. Cut the ends off of each eggplant, then slice each in half lengthwise. Season the eggplant halves with salt and let them sit for 5 minutes. The salt will help absorb the excess liquid inside of the eggplant. After 5 minutes, rinse each eggplant and using paper towels, push out any remaining liquid.

5. Place a large skillet over medium heat, add the oil and preheat, Then add in the eggplant halves and sauté for about 5 minutes or until the eggplant halves are tender and golden. Transfer the halves to a baking sheet, cut side up. Using a spoon, press the flesh down in each eggplant half, making it look like a little ditch. Spoon the stuffing inside of each eggplant.

6. Preheat the oven to 350°F.

7. Prepare the sauce: In a small saucepan over medium heat, add the butter and let it melt, then whisk in the flour and continuously whisk the mixture to prevent it from browning. Whisk in the hot milk and whisk vigorously until the mixture is bubbly. Season with salt, to taste, then remove the sauce from the heat. Add in cheese and eggs and keep stirring until a thickened, creamy white sauce forms.

8. Next, spoon the sauce generously over each eggplant half until the filling is concealed underneath the sauce, Then sprinkle the surface of each eggplant with more Dayia shredded cheddar cheese.

9. Place the eggplant halves in the oven and bake for 5-10 minutes or until the cheese is melted and the sauce is golden. Remove from oven, let sit for 5 minutes, then serve and enjoy!

Greek Fish Florentine

Greek accents transform this mildly-flavored fish into a culinary adventure. Basa is loaded with protein and disease-fighting nutrients. In about 20 minutes you will have a traditional Greek dish that is sure to please everyone.

Yield: 4 (5 oz.) Basa Fillets
Servings: 4 (Serving Size: 1 (5 oz. basa fillet)
Total Time – Prep to Finish: 20 minutes

Ingredients:

- 4 (5oz.) basa fillets
- 10 grape tomatoes, sliced
- 1 clove garlic, sliced thin
- 1 tbsp. fresh Italian-leaf parsley, chopped
- Juice from ½ of a lemon
- 2 large shallots, diced
- 1 tbsp. extra-virgin olive oil
- 8 oz. baby spinach
- 1/4 cup Daiya vegan feta cheese, crumbled

Directions:

1. Preheat oven to 350°F. Place fillets and tomatoes in a glass baking dish. Sprinkle garlic and parsley over top and finish with lemon juice. Cover with foil and bake for 15 to 20 minutes, until fish is opaque and flakes easily with a fork.

2. In a medium skillet over medium-high heat, sauté shallots in oil for 1 minute. Reduce heat to medium and add spinach, cooking until wilted, about 5 minutes. Stir in feta and heat until melted and evenly distributed.

3. To serve, place 3/4 cup spinach-feta mixture on each plate and lay 1 fillet over top, finishing with half of tomatoes.

Briami (Greek Ratatouille)

For a Greek summertime favorite, try Briami (or Greek Ratatouille). Briami is a mixture of vegetables which are cooked in olive oil. The Greek usually make big huge batches of Briami for large parties and celebrations, so many of the traditional Briami recipes you find will yield a very large quantity. Briami is very delicious and satisfying as a main dish course, you will probably find yourself making it often!

Yield: 4-lbs. Briami (8 cups)
Servings: 4 (Serving Size: 2 cups)
Total Time – Prep to Finish: 20 minutes

Ingredients:

- 4 medium sweet potatoes, cut into 2-inch pieces
- 1 cup tomatoes, chopped (or whole cherry tomatoes, if preferred)
- 3-4 eggplants, cut into 2-inch pieces
- 4-5 zucchini, cut into ½-inch slices
- 1-2 onions, cut into quarters
- 2 green bell peppers, cut into slices (opt.)
- 3 cloves garlic, chopped
- 2 tbsp. dry mint, chopped fine
- ¼ c. fresh parsley, chopped fine
- 2 tbsp. fresh oregano, chopped fine
- 2 tbsp. tomato paste
- 1 c. water (to mix with tomato paste)
- 1 c. extra-virgin olive oil
- ½ to ¾ c. water (for pan)
- pinch of salt, or to taste
- pinch of fresh ground black pepper, or to taste

Directions:

1. Preheat oven at 350°F.

2. Begin by washing and patting dry all of the vegetables with paper towel. Then prep the vegetables in manner directed.

3. Place all of the prepped vegetables into a large bowl and add the chopped garlic, mint, parsley, and oregano. Stir gently to mix well.

4. In a small bowl, combine the tomato paste and water. Blend and then mix in with the vegetables.

5. Add ¾ to 1 c. olive oil and mix well with hands.

6. Season with salt and black pepper, to taste.

7. Transfer the vegetables to a large shallow pan; the veggies should be able to fit all in one layer.

8. Pour ½ to ¾ c. water into one of the corners of the pan and tilt the pan just slightly so that it spreads, but not so much that the water pours over the top of the vegetables. Keep a close eye on the water level, adding more if it seems the veggies are becoming dry or the water level too low.

9. Cover the pan with aluminum foil and place in preheated oven to roast for 50-60 minutes or until the vegetables are fork-tender. Cook for longer than 60 minutes if need be, but after the first 60 minutes of roasting, check the veggies frequently as they can quickly go from being perfectly fork-tender to being too mushy.

10. Once the vegetables are fork-tender, remove the foil and continue roasting, uncovered, for 20-30 minutes or until the potatoes are slightly browned and begin to crisp.

11. Remove the Briami from oven and let cool for 10 minutes before serving; garnishing with crumbled feta, if desired. Note: Briami is also often served cold as well as warm. Both ways are simply delicious, but it is typically a personal preference.

Fassolakia Lathera (Green Bean Casserole)

For Greek vegetarians or those on a meat-free diet, Fassolakia Lathera is a popular choice for a filling main dish. "Lathera" refers to vegetarian dishes that are prepred using olive oils and tomatoes. Green beans are one of the most common vegetables used in Lathera-style cooking. However, this dish is versatile and to keep things exciting, especially when using this casserole as a main course, try swapping out the green beans for zucchini, bell peppers, okra, etc. This is a dish that even meat-eaters will enjoy!

Yield: 1 green bean casserole
Servings: 6-8 (Serving Size: 2 cups casserole)
Total Time – Prep to Finish: 1 hour 20 minutes

Ingredients:

- 2-lbs. green beans, clean and trimmed
- ½ c. extra-virgin olive oil
- 1 large onion, diced
- 2 cloves garlic, minced
- 2-3 medium-sized jicama, cut into large wedges
- 1 c. baby carrots
- ½ c. fresh parsley, chopped
- 2 tbsp. tomato paste
- 4-5 ripe tomatoes, skinned and crushed (or 1 can crushed tomatoes)
- 1½ c. warm water
- 1 tsp. coconut palm sugar
- 1 tbsp. fresh dill, chopped
- salt, to taste
- Fresh ground black pepper, to taste

Directions:

1. Place a Dutch oven or large pot over medium-high heat. Add the olive oil and allow it to heat up.

2. Add in the onion and sauté 3-5 minutes or until translucent.

3. Add in the garlic; sauté 2-3 minutes or until fragrant.

4. Add in the green beans, jicama, and carrots. Stir to mix.

5. In a bowl, combine the tomato paste in the water and let it dissolve, then add it to the pot along with the crushed tomato, chopped parsley, and coconut palm sugar. Stir gently to blend.

6. Reduce the heat to medium-low and let simmer for 45-60 minutes , stirring occasionally, or until the green beans are fork-tender, but NOT mushy. Keep a close eye on the level of liquid in the pot while the vegetables are cooking; add more water as needed. During the last 10 minutes of cooking add in the fresh dill and season with salt and black pepper, to taste.

7. Divide among serving plates and serve.

Spanakopita Casserole

Spanakopita, or spinach pie, is a classic fixture in Greek cuisine, most often sold as individual triangular pastries. Enjoy our casserole version as a light snack or appetizer, or pair it with a lentil soup or fresh tomato salad for a more filling main for the whole family.

Yield: 1 casserole
Servings: 6 (Serving Size: 1-2 cups
Total Time – Prep to Finish: 1 hour 15 minutes

Ingredients:

- 1 tsp. extra-virgin olive oil
- 1 tbsp. sweet red pepper, chopped fine
- ¼ c. green onion, chopped fine
- 36 c. fresh spinach, loosely packed
- 1 tbsp. fresh dill, chopped fine
- 1 tsp. fresh mint, chopped fine
- 1 large egg white
- ½ c. Daiya feta, crumbled
- 4 sheets phyllo dough (Using the Phyllo Dough recipe)
- Olive oil cooking spray

Directions:

1. Preheat oven to 375°F. Heat oil in a large sauté pan over medium-high heat. Add pepper and onion and sauté for about 2 minutes. Add spinach in batches, waiting 2 or 3 minutes between intervals; cover tightly and cook, tossing frequently, for about 15 minutes.

2. Drain spinach mixture in a colander, removing any excess liquid, before placing it in a large bowl; set aside. When spinach mixture is cool, mix in dill, mint and egg white. Then fold in feta until well blended. Set aside.

3. Working quickly, roll phyllo out onto a clean work surface. Carefully cut each sheet lengthwise into approximately 4 3-inch-wide pieces. (TIP: Or cut each sheet in half lengthwise, then half each of the 2 sections again to create 4 equal pieces.) Place 3 or 4 strips across the center of a 1 1/2-qt or 9 x 9-inch casserole dish misted with cooking spray, leaving about 3 to 4 inches of excess hanging over on both ends. The strips should be overlapping slightly. Mist strips with cooking spray. Turn the casserole dish clockwise and place 3 or 4 strips across the original layer, at a 90-degree angle. Mist strips with cooking spray. Continue turning and layering until all strips have been used, about 4 layers in total, misting with cooking spray after each layer.

4. Spoon spinach mixture into center of phyllo-covered dish. Fold phyllo hanging over edges into the center of spinach mixture, covering the top (no spinach should be visible). Mist with cooking spray.

5. Bake in preheated oven for 30 to 35 minutes or until lightly brown and crispy. Let casserole sit for 10 to 15 minutes before slicing. Cut into 6 pieces and serve. TIP: Phyllo can be cut with a knife, kitchen scissors or a pizza cutter.

Gyros with Naan Flatbread

Gyros are a Greek dish involving meat that has been roasted to perfection on a vertical spit. It is typically served as a sandwich in flatbread, pita pockets, or naan. It is also commonly served with tomato, onion, and tzatziki sauce. For this recipe we are pairing the gyro meat with naan bread, which is a leavened, oven-baked flatbread. We have also incorporated a delish baba ghanoush dip which adds to the unbeatable flavors of the gyro meat.

Yield: 2-lbs gyro meat; 8 naan flatbreads; 2 c. dip
Servings: 2 (Serving Size: 2 gyros with ¼ c. dip)
Total Time – Prep to Finish: 55 minutes

Ingredients:

For the Gyro Meat:
- 2-lbs. ground lamb
- 1 small yellow onion, chopped
- 8 cloves garlic, divided
- 1 sprig fresh rosemary
- 1 tbsp. dried marjoram

For the Naan Flatbread:
- 5 tbsp. ground flax seeds
- 4 large eggs
- ¾ c. coconut cream (or thick coconut milk)
- ¼ c. extra-virgin olive oil
- ½ c. coconut flour
- 1 c. arrowroot powder
- 1 ½ tsp. baking powder
- ½ tsp. sea salt
- 1 tsp. Vinegar
- Coconut oil or ghee for cooking

For the BabaGhanoush Dip:
- 3 medium-sized eggplants
- 2 cloves garlic
- ½ c. tahini
- juice of ½ of a large lemon
- sea salt, to taste
- avocado oil

For the Cucumber Sauce (opt.):
- 1 large cucumber, peeled and chopped
- 1 tbsp. extra-virgin olive oil
- 1 tbsp. lemon juice
- 4 fresh mint leaves
- 1 small tomato, chopped, to garnish

Directions:

1. Prepare the Naan Flatbread: Place the naan ingredients into a food processor in the order listed; pulse until contents are well blended.

2. Place a large skillet over medium-high heat and add the 1-2 tbsp. of the coconut oil (or ghee). Allow it to melt, then add about ¼ c. of naan batter to the skillet. Quickly wet your finger with water and tap the batter down to help it spread into the shape of a circle (Do this with caution as the skillet will be hot to the touch, so be sure to touch only the dough – do not touch the surface of the skillet itself). Cook for 2 minutes or until golden and then flip and continue cooking for about 2 more minutes or until the second side is golden in color and the naan bread is cooked through.

3. Prepare the Gyro Meat: To begin place a cast iron, heavy-bottomed skillet over medium heat. Add in the meat and cook until the meat has browned. Transfer the meat to a bowl and then immediately add the onion to the empty, hot skillet and sauté for 5 minutes. Add in 4 cloves of the garlic; sauté for 1 minute. Add in the rosemary and marjoram. Stir to incorporate, then turn off the 4.   heat, cover the skillet with a lid and let rest for about 5 minutes. After 5 minutes has passes, place the meat back into the skillet and stir to blend with the onion and the garlic.

4. Prepare the Cucumber Sauce (Opt.): In a food processor, combine the cucumber, remaining 4 cloves of garlic, olive oil, lemon juice, and fresh mint leaves. Process until contents are well blended. Set aside.

5. Prepare the Baba Ghanoush Dip: Before preparing the meat and naan, prepare the Baba Ghanoush dip as it takes the longest amount of time to prepare.. First preheat oven to 400°F and line a baking sheet with parchment paper. Next, cut the eggplants in half and rub each of the halves with avocado oil. Place the eggplant halves cut-side down on the parchment-lined baking sheet.

6. Place the 2 garlic cloves in the corners of the baking sheet and bake for about 35 minutes or until the eggplant is soft and the garlic is browned. Remove from the oven and let cool for about 15 minutes. With a large metal spoon, scoop out the inside flesh of the eggplant halves and place them in a food processor. Process until smooth then remover the browned garlic skins from the cloves of roasted garlic and then add the garlic, along with the lemon juice and tahini, to the food processor. Pulse until just blended, but not completely smooth. Season with salt to taste.

7. To Serve: Divide the gyro meat among the 8 pieces of naan flatbread (2 pieces of flatbread per serving). Place the gyro meat into the center of each flatbread. If using the cucumber sauce, drizzle it over the meat on each flatbread now. Top the meat with chopped tomato, to garnish (if desired). Serve the gyros with ¼-½ c. of the Baba Ghanoush dip and then serve and enjoy!

Moussaka

Greek-style lasagna that uses layers of eggplant, a spicy meat filling, and a creamy béchamel sauce. This is Greek comfort food at its finest – we just added a healthier spin on a Greek great!

Yield: 6 to 8 (4 x 3-inch) servings
Servings: 2 (Serving Size: 11 oz. serving – about a 4 x 3-inch piece)
Total Time – Prep to Finish: 1 hour 35 minutes

Ingredients:

For the Eggplant:
- 2 medium eggplants (about 2-lbs.)
- Extra-virgin olive oil
- Fine-grain sea salt, to taste
- Fresh ground black pepper, to taste

For the Béchamel Sauce:
- ¾ c. almond milk (or coconut milk)
- 2 c. cauliflower florets
- 1 clove garlic, minced
- 1 tsp. fine-grain sea salt, or to taste
- pinch fresh ground black pepper, or to taste
- 3 large eggs

For the Meat Filling:
- 1-lb. ground lamb (or lean beef, if preferred)
- 1 tbsp. extra-virgin olive oil
- 1 medium onion, chopped fine
- 1 garlic clove, minced
- 1 (28 oz.) can diced tomatoes
- 1 c. arrowroot powder
- 2 tsp. dried oregano
- 1 tsp. ground cinnamon
- 1 tbsp. red vinegar
- fresh parsley, chopped, to garnish

Directions:
1. Preheat oven to 400°F (200°C), place a rack in the middle.
2. Prepare the Eggplant: Wash eggplants; pat dry with paper towel. Peel and slice each eggplant into ½-inch rounds. On a baking sheet, toss the eggplant slices with the olive oil and season generously with salt and pepper. Arrange the slices on the baking sheet in a single layer and roast in the oven for 25-30 minutes or until soft and golden. Prepare the meat filling.
3. Prepare the Meat Filling: In a large saucepan over medium-high heat, add 1 tbsp. of olive oil. Add the onion and garlic; sauté 2-3 minutes or until onion is translucent. Add the

meat; cook, stirring, for 5-7 minutes or until browned through. Stir in the diced tomatoes, tomato paste, parsley, oregano, cinnamon, vinegar, salt & pepper. Simmer 15-20 minutes, turn off heat and set aside.

4. Prepare the Béchamel Sauce: In a saucepan, combine the cauliflower florets, almond milk, garlic, salt and pepper; stir to blend. Bring contents to a boil; reduce heat, simmer, covered, for 15 minutes. Transfer the sauce to a blender or food processor, process until smooth. Add in the eggs, one at a time, working quickly making sure that they don't begin to poach. The sauce will look like a thin white foamy liquid, this is fine.

5. Assemble the Moussaka: Lightly grease an 8 x12-inch baking dish (or individual ramekins) Add the sliced eggplant to form a uniform bottom layer. Cover the eggplant layer evenly with half of the meat mixture. Repeat process to make a second layer. Carefully spoon the cauliflower béchamel sauce over the meat mixture and spread the sauce evenly to the edges (try not to disturb the meat mixture as much as possible). Place in the oven and bake the moussaka uncovered for 20-25 minutes or until the top is browned and puffed. Remove from the oven and let sit for 10 minutes, then sprinkle with fresh chopped parsley, to garnish, and serve!

Tsigaridia (Greek pork belly)

Pork belly is a worthy addition to many Greek dishes, from appetizers to side dishes to main dishes, pork belly is often used as a healthier, yet equally delicious, alternative to bacon. In Greek cooking, pork belly is referred to as Tsigaridia. It is simple to make and is a meat that the entire family will love.

Yield: 2-lbs. Tsigaridia
Servings: 4 (Serving Size: 6-8 oz.)
Total Time – Prep to Finish: 20 minutes

Ingredients:

- 2-lbs of pork belly
- 4 tbsp. extra-virgin olive oil, for frying
- Juice of 2 large lemons
- 2 tbsp. oregano
- Sea salt, to taste
- Fresh ground black pepper, to taste

Directions:

1. First, wash the pork belly. Then, using a sharp knife, remove the thick pork skin on the one side, if the pork was sold with the skin intact. Finally, cut the pork belly into 1-inch cubes.

2. Place a large skillet over medium heat; add the olive oil. Add the pork cubes to the hot oil and fry, stirring often, for 8-10 minutes or until the pork is browned and cooked-through. When the pork is nearly done, add the oregano and lemon juice. Stir to incorporate. Finally, add the sea salt and black pepper, to taste. Stir.

3. Transfer the pork to plates or incorporate into desired recipe. Serve.

Greek Slovaki with Grilled Vegetables

Souvlaki is a popular Greek fast food consisting of small, tender pieces of meat. It is very versatile and can be seen rolled in appetizers, served as snacks, grilled on skewers for a tasty lunch, served with vegetables for a filling dinner, and much more. For this recipe, we are using slovaki as a delicious, satisfying dinner, pairing the meat with tender, grilled vegetables. You may want to double the recipes, because there will be requests for seconds, and maybe even thirds of this mouthwatering Greek meat dish.

Yield: 12 slovaki (meat) kabobs; 12 vegetable skewers
Servings: 8 (Serving Size: 3 slovaki (meat) kabobs; 3 vegetable skewers)
Total Time – Prep to Finish: 25 minutes (Inactive time: 5-6 hours needed for marinating meat)
Ingredients:

- 2-lbs. trimmed steak or lamb, cut into 1½-inch cubes
- 1 c. red bell pepper, cut into 1½-inch pieces
- 1 c. green bell pepper, cut into 1½-inch pieces
- 4 small onions (1½-inch diameter or less)
- 2 c. yellow squash(1.5" thick slices)
- 6 tbsp. extra virgin olive oil
- juice of 1 lemon (about 1 tbsp.)
- 2 tbsp. white vinegar
- 4 small cloves garlic, minced
- 2 tsp. dried oregano
- 4 small bay leaves, crushed

Directions:

1. If using wooden skewers, first soak them in cool water for 20 minutes before grilling to prevent charring.

2. First, combine the olive oil, lemon juice, vinegar, minced garlic, dried oregano, and crushed bay leaves in a gallon-sized sealable Ziploc plastic bag. Place the cubed meat into the plastic bag, seal, and shake the bag to coat the meat well with the marinade. Place the sealed bag in the refrigerator and allow the meat to marinate for 4-5 hours. Occasionally shake the bag to re-coat the meat with the marinade.

3. When the meat is nearly finished marinating, prepare the vegetables as directed, then parboil the peppers for 1 minute; remove from the water. Add in the squash and parboil for 2-3 minutes; remove from the water. Add in the onions; parboil 3-4 minutes, then remove from the water. Do not leave the vegetables in the water for longer than as directed.

4. Preheat the grill to medium heat. Spray the grates with high-heat cooking spray.

5. Place the vegetables on to 12 skewers and brush the skewered vegetables with olive oil and then sprinkle on a pinch of dried oregano. Season the vegetable with salt and pepper, if desired. Next, skewer the meat onto 12 skewers.

6. Grill the meat and vegetables skewers for 5-10 minutes, turning sides often until the meat is cooked through and the vegetables are nicely browned and fork tender.

7. Place 3 meat and 3 vegetable skewers onto each serving plate and serve immediately with tzatziki sauce or another preferred sauce/dip, if desired.

GREEK SNACKS/DESSERTS

Baklava

Popular in Greece and throughout the Middle East, baklava is a rich, sweet pastry made using layers of crust (typically filo dough) and filling the flaky dough layers with chopped nuts, such as walnuts and pistachios, sweet syrups or honey, and a variety of spices. Baklava is a delicious Mediterranean dessert that the whole family can agree on!

Yield: 8 stuffed eggplant halves
Servings: 8 (Serving Size: half an eggplant with filling)
Total Time – Prep to Finish: 45 minutes

Ingredients:

For the Dough Layers:
- 1/4 cup Grass Fed Butter, Melted
- 2 large eggs
- ¼ tsp. sea salt
- ¾ c. coconut flout

For the Syrup:
- ½ c. honey
- ½ c. water
- 1 tbsp. cinnamon
- 1 tsp. cloves
- Lemon zest, to taste

For the Filling:
- 2 tbsp. coconut butter, melted
- ½ c. dates, pitted and chopped
- 2 tbsp. honey
- 1 c. walnuts (or preferred nuts) chopped
- 1 tbsp. cinnamon
- 1 tsp. cloves
- ½ tsp. vanilla extract

Directions:

1. Preheat the oven to 325°F.
2. Prepare the dough layers. In a mixing bowl, combine the dough layer ingredients in the order listed; mix together until contents are well blended. The dough will be crumbly. Take half of the dough out of the mixing bowl and place it between 2 sheets of parchment paper. Using a rolling pin, roll the dough out to be as thin as possible. Take the flattened crust layer out of the parchment paper and lay it in the bottom of a baking dish. Roll out the remaining half of the dough in the same manner; but set the second sheet of dough off to the side until needed.

3. Prepare the Baklava Filling: In a mixing bowl, combine all of the filling ingredients in the order listed. Blend until well incorporated and then spread the filling evenly across the layer of dough in the baking dish. Place the reserved layer of dough onto the dough with the filling and pat the dough down evenly. Brush the top with more melted coconut oil and then cut and place the baking dish into the preheated oven for 15-20 minutes or until lightly golden. Watch the baking closely so that the baklava does not burn.

4. Prepare the Syrup: In a small saucepan over low heat, combine the syrup ingredients in the order listed and blend well. Cook for 10 minutes.

5. Remove the baklava from the oven and pour the syrup evenly over the surface of the baklava. Cover and place the baklava in the freezer until it has stiffened. Then serve and enjoy!

Galaktoboureko (Greek Custard Pie)

Like baklava, Galaktoboureko is another very popular Greek dessert. It can be found in most restaurants, bakeries, pastry shops, and almost anywhere else sweets are sold throughout Greece. Galaktoboureko is made by layering phyllo dough with a sweet, creamy custard filling. A delicious and fun dessert that the whole family will love – have the kids help in the preparation of this cherished part of Greek culture!

Yield: about 24 pieces
Servings: 24 (Serving Size: 1 piece)
Total Time – Prep to Finish: 1 hour 30 minutes

Ingredients:

For the Custard Filling:

- 6 c. almond milk
- 1¼ c. coarse ground almond meal
- 6 egg yolks
- ½ c. coconut palm sugar
- 1 tbsp. vanilla extract
- 2 tbsp. grass-fed butter (or coconut oil), softened

For the Syrup:

- 1 c. coconut palm sugar
- 1 cup water
- 2-inch piece of lemon rind
- 2-inch piece of orange rind
- Juice of ½ a lemon

For the Phyllo Dough:

- 1 lb. phyllo pastry sheet (follow Phyllo Recipe in the Appetizers/Snacks Section)

For the Finishing Touches:

- 1/2 lb. grass-fed butter (or coconut oil), melted (for brushing)

Directions:

1. Prepare the Filling: Place a large saucepan over medium-high heat, add in the almond milk and just barely bring the milk to a boil, then add the almond meal and whisk well to blend. Reduce heat to medium-low.

2. In a separate bowl, combine the egg yolks and coconut palm sugar; beat until the sugar has mostly dissolved then ladle a cup of the warmed almond milk into the egg-sugar mixture to temper. Then transfer egg-sugar mixture to the saucepan with the almond milk. Stir to incorporate. Cook over medium-low heat, stirring frequently, for 10-15 minutes or until the cream begins to thicken into a custard-like consistency. When the custard has thickened, remove from the heat and stir in the vanilla extract and the butter. Set aside.

3. Prepare the Phyllo Dough Sheets: as directed in the recipe and cut the sheets to make

stacks of 9 x 12-inch sheets. To prevent drying, cover one stack with wax paper and a damp paper towel while working with the other.

4. Preheat the oven to 350°F.

5. Assemble the Galaktoboureko: Using a pastry brush, brush the bottom and sides of a 9 x 12 rectangular pan. You will use approximately half the phyllo sheets for the bottom of the pastry. Begin by layering the phyllo sheets one by one in the bottom of the pan, brushing each sheet thoroughly with the melted butter. When you have almost layered half of the phyllo sheets, drape two sheets of phyllo so that they extend half in the pan and half out of the pan horizontally.

6. Next, add the custard in an even layer on top of the sheets, smoothing the surface with a rubber spatula. Fold the phyllo sheet flaps in over the custard layer. Add the remaining sheets on top, brushing each sheet with melted butter. Before baking, score the top layer of phyllo (making sure not to puncture the filling layer) to enable easier cutting of pieces later.

7. Place the Galaktoboureko in the preheated oven and bake for 40-45 minutes or until the phyllo turns a deep golden color. While the Galaktoboureko is baking, prepare the syrup.

8. Prepare the Syrup: In a saucepan over medium-high heat, combine the coconut palm sugar and water. Stir until the sugar is dissolved, then add in the lemon peel and orange peel. Bring contents to a boil and allow it to boil for approximately 10 – 15 minutes. Remove the lemon and orange peels and stir in the lemon juice. Remove the saucepan from the heat and set aside to cool.

9. Remove the Galaktoboureko from the oven; let cool to room temperature. Slice and place a piece of the Galaktoboureko onto a serving plate, then ladle with room temperature syrup, allow the syrup to absorb into the layers for a couple of minutes, and then serve and enjoy!

Amygthalota: Almond Cookies

These almond cookies, referred to in Greece as Amygthalota, are a very popular part of Greek tradition. They are made mostly with almonds, which is what makes up most of the dough. This can make the dough more difficult to work with, but the secret is to keep your hands well-oiled with sunflower seed oil or another type of seed oil while forming the cookies. This will keep the dough from being too sticky or too grainy/loose to form.

Yield: about 24-30 cookies
Servings: 12-15 (Serving Size: 2 cookies)
Total Time – Prep to Finish: 40 minutes

Ingredients:

For the Almond Cookies:

- 3 egg whites
- 1 c. coconut palm sugar
- 1½ -lbs blanched almonds, chopped fine – not pulverized)
- 2 tbsp. breadcrumbs, toasted (see recipe)
- 3 tablespoons of freshly squeezed lemon juice
- 2 tablespoons of blanched almond flour
- ½ tsp. baking powder
- Pinch of salt
- baking parchment paper (optional)
- a little seed oil for hands and parchment

For the Breadcrumbs:

- ½ c. almond meal (or almond flour)
- ¼ c. golden flaxseed meal
- 1 tsp. garlic powder
- ½ tsp. onion powder
- ½ tsp. thyme
- ½ tsp. dried oregano
- 1¼ tsp. sea salt
- ½ tsp. fresh ground black pepper

Directions:

1. Preheat oven to 340°F. Line a cookie sheet with parchment paper; lightly oil the parchment paper with sunflower seed oil.

2. Prepare the breadcrumbs. Mix the breadcrumb ingredients in the order listed. Mix well. Toast 2 tbsp. of the breadcrumbs and then set aside. Place the blanched almonds in a food processor; process to chop fine, but DO NOT pulverize. Set aside.

3. In a large bowl, beat the egg whites and coconut palm sugar until frothy.

4. Using a wooden spoon, stir the chopped blanched almonds, breadcrumbs, lemon juice, blanched almond flour, baking powder, and salt into the egg white mixture. Stir until the ingredients are well incorporated. The dough won't be smooth – it will be similar in comparison to rice in melted marshmallow.

5. Lightly oil hands with the sunflower seed oil or another type of seed oil. Take a large handful of the dough and form it into a cohesive mass. Form the dough into flattened log-shaped cookies that are approximately 1-inch across and 3-inches long. Place the formed cookies onto the greased parchment-lined cookie sheet and place in the preheated oven. Bake for 25-30 minutes or until the golden crisp, yet chewy. Keep a watchful eye on the cookies during baking as they can go from being perfectly golden to being burnt very quickly. When the cookies have finished baking, place them on wire racks to cool before serving.

Melomakarona (Honey Spice Cookies)

Melomakarona cookies are a classic Christmas time tradition throughout Greece. They are oil-based and result in a chewy, super moist, cake-like cookie. They are flavored with brandy and orange and dipped in a sweet honey-sugar syrup, then sprinkled with walnuts. Make a bunch, because these cookies are sure to be a big hit!

Yield: approx. 60 cookies
Servings: 30 (Serving Size: 2 cookies)
Total Time – Prep to Finish: 55 minutes

Ingredients:

For the Cookies:

- 1 c. extra-virgin olive oil
- 1 c. canola oil
- ¾ c. coconut palm sugar
- Zest of one orange
- ¾ c. fresh-squeezed orange juice (2-3 oranges)
- ¼ c. cooking brandy
- 2 tsp. baking powder
- 1 tsp. baking soda
- Pinch of salt
- 7½ c. coconut flour (or almond flour)
- ¾ c. walnuts, ground coarsely
- Ground cinnamon, to garnish

For the Syrup:

- 1 c. honey
- 1 c. coconut palm sugar
- 1½ c. water
- 1 cinnamon stick
- 3-4 whole cloves
- 1 to 2-inch piece of a lemon rind
- 1 tsp. fresh-squeezed lemon juice

Directions:

1. Preheat the oven to 350°F.

2. In a small bowl, combine the orange zest and coconut palm sugar, using your fingers to rub the grains of orange zest just as you would rub sand between your fingers) in order to release the oils from the orange zest into the sugar. Using an electric hand mixer, beat in the olive oil with the orange-sugar mixture until contents are well blended.

3. In a separate mixing bowl, sift the flour with the baking powder, baking soda, and salt.

Add the orange juice and brandy to the mixing bowl and mix well.

4. Slowly incorporate the flour mixture, 1 cup at a time, until a dough the forms. The dough should not be that is not too loose nor too firm - It will be dense and wet, but not sticky. Once the flour is incorporated fully, stop mixing.

5. Pinch off a portion of the dough that is about the size of a walnut. Using your hands, shape the dough into a small, smooth, egg-shaped piece. Place the formed dough on an ungreased cookie sheet. Repeat with remaining dough. You should have about 60 cookies. Use a second cookie sheet, if needed. Press the tines of a large fork in a criss-cross pattern in the center of each cookie. This will flatten them slightly in the center. The cookies should resemble lightly flattened ovals when they go in the oven. Place the cookies in the preheated oven and bake for 25 – 30 minutes until lightly browned.

6. While the cookies are baking, prepare the syrup by placing a saucepan over medium-high heat. Add in the honey, coconut palm sugar, water, cinnamon, cloves, and the lemon rind. Bring contents to a boil, stirring very often, then reduce heat and let simmer, uncovered, for 10-15 more minutes. Remove the cinnamon, cloves, and the lemon rind and then stir in the lemon juice.

7. Place the ground walnuts in a shallow bowl next to the stove top. When the cookies come out of the oven and while they are still very warm, carefully float the cookies in the syrup and allow the cookies to absorb syrup on both sides. Using a small spatula, remove the cookie from the syrup and place the cookie on a plate. Press ground walnuts lightly into the tops of the cookies (syrup will help it adhere) and then lightly sprinkle the cookies with ground cinnamon. Do not store cookies in the refrigerator, they will harden. Instead, store the cookies in an airtight container at room temperature.

Vasilopita Cake

This cake was created originally to honor the feast of Saint Basil the Great, thus the name "Vasilopita" meaning 'St. Basil's Bread." – In Greek tradition, it is a cake often made to celebrate the ringing in of each New Year. Throughout Greece, this New Year's cake can be seen at most New Year's and other various celebrations. This is a simple, moist bread cake that is topped with lemon juice and chopped or slivered nuts.

Yield: 1 vasilopita cake
Servings: 8-10 (Serving Size: 1 slice of vasilopita)
Total Time – Prep to Finish: 1 hour 20 minutes

Ingredients:

- 1 c. grass-fed butter or coconut oil, softened
- 2 c. coconut palm sugar
- 3 c. coconut flour (or almond flour)
- 6 eggs
- 2 tsp. baking powder (or arrowroot powder)
- 1 c. coconut milk, warmed to 110°F (or almond milk)
- ½ tsp. baking soda
- 1 tbsp. fresh-squeezed lemon juice
- ¼ c. blanched slivered almonds (or preferred nuts, chopped or slivered)
- 2 tbsp. coconut palm sugar, or as needed

Directions:

1. Preheat oven to 350°F. Grease a 10-inch round cake pan generously with cooking spray.

2. In a medium-sized mixing bowl, cream together the butter (or coconut oil) and 2 c. coconut palm sugar. Stir in the coconut flour and blend until the mixture is grain-like. Add in the eggs, one at a time, blending the eggs into the mixture after adding each one.

3. In a separate small bowl, combine the warmed milk and baking powder. Whisk well to blend. Add the milk mixture to the flour-egg mixture, mix until well incorporated.

4. In another small bowl, combine the lemon juice and baking soda; mix well. Add to batter.

5. Pour the batter into prepared cake pan, tap the pan gently on the counter to smooth the batter out. Place in the preheated oven and bake for 20 minutes. Remove and sprinkle the top of the cake with the nuts and the 2 tbsp. coconut palm sugar. Place the cake back into the oven and bake for 20-30 more minutes or until a toothpick inserted into the center of the cake comes out clean. Let cool for 10 minutes, then slice and serve!

6. Note: to follow tradition: gently cut a small hole into the cake. Place a quarter in the hole. Cover the quarter and hole with sugar. Place the cake on a wire rack to cool for 10 minutes. After 10 minutes, invert onto a plate. Slice and serve the cake warm. Each family member gets a slice of cake, beginning with the youngest member being served first. Whichever family member ends up with the quarter in their slice of cake will have good luck the whole year long!

Koulourakia Ouzou: Traditional Ouzo Cookies

The Greek tradition of using olive oil to make cookies and other treats is centuries old. There is a long list of these olive-oil based cookies, Koulourakia Ouzou is a very popular type of olive oil cookie. The flavor of Greece cooking is abundant in these delicious, crispy, yet perfectly chewy cookies. These cookies are typically shaped into either a rolled dough design or formed into little mounds. The recipes typically yield many cookies as they are traditionally used to feed many people at parties and celebrations, more so than just one family at home, so you can either abide by the large recipes and freeze what you don't use or adjust the recipe to yield a more appropriate amount to better meet your own personal needs.

Yield: about 100 cookies
Servings: 50 (Serving Size: 2 cookies)
Total Time – Prep to Finish: 30 minutes

Ingredients:

- ½ c. extra-virgin olive oil
- 1 c. coconut palm sugar
- 2 large eggs
- ¼ c. Greek ouzo liqueur
- ¼ tsp. ground anise and ¼ tsp. ground coriander combined
- juice of ½ a lemon
- 5½ c. blanched almond flour
- 1 tsp. baking powder
- a pinch of salt
- sesame seeds (opt.)

Directions:

1. Preheat oven to 390°F. Line several cookies sheets with parchment paper.

2. In a small bowl, combine ¼ tsp. ground anise and ¼ tsp. ground coriander and mix well to yield ½ tsp. of the blended seasonings.

3. In a large mixing bowl, combine the olive oil, coconut palm sugar, and eggs. Whisk until the mixture is light and creamy. Then beat in the ouzo liqueur, the blended anise and coriander seasonings, and the lemon juice. Whisk until the batter is well blended.

4. In a separate bowl, combine the blanched almond flour and baking powder. Whisk well to combine, and then add it to the batter, stirring and kneading the cookie dough until the dough is smooth and elastic and no longer sticks to the sides of the bowl.

5. On a work surface, using well-oiled hands, roll small pieces of the dough into strips and then twist or coil the dough to form the shape of a cookie. If using sesame seeds, roll the dough through a few scattered sesame seeds before forming into a cookie. Place the formed cookie onto one of the parchment-lined cookie sheets. Repeat with remaining dough to form the rest of the cookies. Arrange the cookies on the cookie sheets so that there is about an inch or two of space between them.

6. Place the cookie sheets in the preheated oven and bake for 25-30 minutes or until golden. Remove from oven and let cool on wire racks before serving.

Firikia Glyko: Whole Apples in Light Syrup

Firikia Glyko are Greek spoon sweets which consist of small apples which are cooked in a light syrup with cinnamon and cloves to create a delicious and traditional treat. Spoon sweets are a traditional and delightful Greek custom which involved the offering of spoon sweets to guests as a symbol of hospitality. They are called spoon sweets because the usual serving size is a well-filled teaspoon. According to legend, guests would use teaspoons and partake from the same bowl in order to assure that the food was not poisoned and safe for all to eat.

Yield: about 24 small apples
Servings: 24 (Serving Size: 1 small apple)
Total Time – Prep to Finish: 1 hour 15 minutes

Ingredients:

- 5½-lbs. (about 24 total) sweet, small apples (preferably firikia, if available), peeled
- 48 whole cloves (2 for each apple)
- 11 c. coconut palm sugar
- 10½ c. water
- 2 sticks of cinnamon
- ½ c. brandy
- juice of 1 large lemon (about 3-4 tbsp.)

Directions:

1. Peel the apples.

2. Place one clove in the top and one clove in the bottom of each peeled apple.

3. In a large pot or Dutch oven over medium-high heat, combine the coconut palm sugar, water, and 2 sticks of cinnamon. Stir well to blend and to dissolve the sugar. Bring contents to a boil, stirring occasionally with a wooden spoon. When a full-boil is achieved, reduce heat to low or medium-low to maintain a light boil and then let cook, uncovered, for 1 hour 15 minutes.

4. When there is 5 minutes of cooking time left, blend the brandy and lemon juice together in a small bowl and add to the boiling apples. Stir to blend.

5. Remove the apples from the heat and allow them to cool in the pot completely or until lightly warm to the touch. Using a slotted spoon, carefully remove the apples and place one apple on each serving plate. Drizzle a little syrup over each apple and serve!

Kerasi Glyko tou Koutaliou: Cherry Spoon Sweet

Another popular Greek Spoon Sweet is called Kerasi Glyko tou Koutaliou (also referred to in English as the "Cherry Spoon Sweet." The recipe is simple, using only four ingredients, yet the taste is phenominal. Kerasi Glyko tou Koutaliou combines firm cherries, sugar, lemon juice, and vanilla extract – this is the most colorful of all the Greek Spoon Sweets, turning a bright, vibrant red when finished.

Yield: 2¾-lbs. cherries
Servings: about 25 (Serving Size: 1 heaping teaspoonful)
Total Time – Prep to Finish: 40 minutes

Ingredients:

- 2¾-lbs. fresh firm cherries (slightly under-ripe)
- 6 1/4 cups of granulated sugar
- 1 teaspoon of lemon juice
- 1/2 teaspoon of vanilla etract (optional)

Directions:

1. Begin by washing the cherries very well. Remove the stems. Push out the pits very carefully using a cherry pitter, cherry stoner, or large sewing needle, making sure to leave the fruit intact. Discard pits and stems. Place the cherries in a colander and set aside to drain.

2. Place a large pot or Dutch oven over medium heat. Combine the coconut palm sugar and water; blend well and then bring mixture to a boil (about 5-10 minutes), stirring frequently to prevent the mixture from sticking to the bottom of the pot. When the syrup reaches a consistency similar to maple syrup, remove the pot from the heat and let the mixture cool slightly.

3. Add the cherries to the mixture, stirring gently to coat the cherries in the syrup, and then increase heat to high. Bring contents to a boil (about 5-10 minutes). Using a slotted spoon, skim any foam as it rises off the surface of the mixture. Stir in lemon juice. Allow the mixture to boil for 1 more minute, add vanilla extract (if using), and then remove the cherries from the heat. Let cool completely.

4. To serve, plate 1 heaping teaspoonful of the cherries and the syrup onto a small plate. Traditionally Kerasi Glyko tou Koutaliou is always served with a glass of cold water. Store any remaining cherries/syrup in airtight glass jars.

Pantespani: Greek Sponge Cake

This is a traditional recipe for Pantespani, a light sponge cake, soaked in a light syrup. It can be served as is, with toppings, and without the syrup as any other sponge cake. The tastes of orange, cloves, and cinnamon give it a lovely taste and fabulous aroma. The recipe is easy and calls for self-rising flour.

Yield: about 100 cookies
Servings: 50 (Serving Size: 2 cookies)
Total Time – Prep to Finish: 30 minutes

Ingredients:

For the Cake:

- 6 eggs, separated
- 2 c. coconut palm sugar, divided
- pinch of salt
- 3 tablespoons of arrowroot powder
- 2 cups blanched almond flour
- 3 tsp. baking powder
- ½ tsp. Salt
- 3 tbsp. orange zest, grated
- 2/3 c. of water
- Coconut oil, melted (or cooking spray)
- Coconut flour, for dusting cake pan

For the Syrup:

- 3 c. water
- 1 c. coconut palm sugar
- 3-4 whole cloves
- 1 stick of cinnamon
- 2 tbsp. brandy

Directions:

1. In a saucepan over medium heat, combine all of the syrup ingredients except for the orange juice and brandy. Bring contents to a boil; boil for 7-8 minutes. Stir in orange juice and brandy, remove from heat, and allow to cool.

2. Preheat oven to 340°F

3. In a mixing bowl, combine the egg whites along with ½ c. of the coconut palm sugar, and the pinch of salt. Using an electric hand mixer, beat contents until stiff peaks form

4. In a separate mixing bowl, beat the egg yolks with the remaining 1½ c. of coconut palm sugar. In another mixing bowl, combine the blanched almond flour, the baking powder, and the ½ tsp. salt. Blend well, and then beat into the bowl with the egg yolk mixture.

5. Then slowly beat in the orange zest and 2/3 c. water. Blend together thoroughly, using a spatula to scrape down the sides of the mixing bowl, and when all ingredients have mixed in, beat on medium-high speed for 3-4 minutes. Using a spatula, gently fold the egg white mixture into the bowl with the egg yolks and stir until well blended.

6. Using melted coconut oil (or cooking spray), lightly grease the bottom and sides of a 15¾ X

64

12 inch (or equivalent) cake pan and then dust with coconut flour. Pour the cake batter to the prepared pan, tapping the pan gently on the countertop a couple of times to smooth out the top and evenly distribute the batter. Place the cake pan in the preheated oven and bake for 55-60 minutes or until a knife inserted into the center of the cake comes out dry. The top should be golden in color. Remove from oven and let cool. To serve, place a slice of cake on each serving plate and drizzle with the syrup.

Caveman Cookbooks
PALEO GRILLING RECIPES
By Angela Anottacelli

GRILLED MEAT & SEAFOOD RECIPES

Grilled Prawns with Banana Salsa

In the mood for a tropical treat for dinner? Well, here is a light and satisfying dish that centers around golden grilled prawns and a sweet, tangy, (and a little spicy!) banana-based salsa.

Yield: 4 giant prawns (or 8 regular-sized prawns) and 2 c. salsa
Servings: 4 (Serving Size: 1 giant prawn (or 2 regular-sized prawns) and ½ c. salsa)
Total Time – Prep to Finish: 30 minutes

Ingredients:
For the Prawns:
- 4 giant prawns (or 8 regular prawns)
- Zest from 1-2 limes
- Juice from 1-2 limes
- Drizzle of olive oil, or as needed

For the Banana Salsa:
- 2 bananas, thinly sliced
- 2 cucumbers, peeled, seeded and diced
- 4 small sweet peppers, diced
- ½ c. fresh cilantro, chopped plus some to garnish
- 8-10 mint leaves, chopped, plus some to garnish
- Juice from 2 limes

Directions:
1. Prepare the Prawns: Place te lime zest and juice into a bowl along with a little olive oil; stir to mix well and then place the prawns in the bowl to marinate for 30 minutes. Make sure to turn the prawns often in the marinade so that all sides are evenly marinated.

2. Preheat the grill (or grill pan) to medium-high heat.

3. Transfer the prawns to the preheated grill and grill for 5-7 minutes per side for large prawns and 3-4 minutes per side for small-regular-sized prawns. . The prawns will become pink in color as they cook. Be careful to not overcook the prawns or the meat will dry out and lose its flavor.

4. Transfer the cooked prawns to a clean, dry plate. If the prawns are already deveined, then prepare the salsa.

5. If the prawns are not deveined then devein the prawns by first removing the outer, hard shell and using a sharp knife, slice a slit down the back of the prawn (or the longer side of the prawn), Then carefully scrape out the dark-colored vein. Set aside and prepare the salsa.

6. Prepare the Banana Salsa: Prepare the ingredients as directed and place the banana, cucumber, sweet peppers, cilantro, and mint into a medium-sized mixing bowl. Drizzle the lime juice over the salsa ingredients. Toss/stir to mx, so that the contents are evenly

coated in lime.

7. To serve, place 1 large prawn (or 2 regular-sized prawns) on a serving dish along ½ c. of banana salsa and a sprig of cilantro or a few mint leaves, to garnish.

Honey-Mustard Salmon with Grilled Asparagus

Flaky and flavorful salmon filets rubbed with a honey-mustard glaze and served with a side of grilled asparagus. This is a delectable dish that is enjoyably fulfilling. Incredibly simple and quick to make with very few ingredients needed, but the taste is gourmet and the presentation sophisticated.

Yield: 4 (6 oz.) salmon fillets; 1-lb. asparagus; 2 c. horseradish sauce
Servings: 2 (Serving Size: 1 (6 oz.) salmon fillet; ¼-lb. asparagus)
Total Time – Prep to Finish: 25 minutes

Ingredients:
For the Grilled Salmon & Asparagus:
- 4 (6 oz.) salmon fillets
- sea salt, to taste
- fresh ground black pepper, to taste
- 2 tbsp. Dijon mustard
- 2 tbsp. Honey
- 1/2 tsp. horseradish (see recipe)
- 1-pound asparagus, trimmed
- 2 tbsp. extra virgin olive oil, divided

For the Horseradish Sauce (Yield: 1 cup):
- 2 c. fresh horseradish root peeled and diced
- 1/3 c. water
- 4 Tbsp. white wine vinegar
- 1 tsp. sea salt

Directions:
1. Prepare the Horseradish Sauce: Using a sharp paring knife or vegetable peeler, remove the tough outer layer from the horseradish root. Take about a 6-inch section from the root and chop it into small pieces. Transfer the pieces of the root to a food processor and add in 1/3 c. water. Pulse until the contents are ground and have formed a pulp. Transfer to a medium-size bowl and stir in the vinegar and salt until well blended. If you want the sauce to be extra hot, add the vinegar right when you transfer the horseradish from te food processor to the bowl. However, if you want a more mild tasting sauce, let the horseradish rest in the bowl for 5 minutes before adding in the vinegar. Reserve 1 tsp. of the sauce from the bowl and then transfer the remaining sauce to an airtight jar with lid to store and use as needed. Stays fresh for up to 6 weeks.

2. Preheat grill to medium low.

3. Prepare the Grilled Salmon and Grilled Asparagus: First, season salmon filets with sea salt

71

and black pepper.

4. In a small-sized mixing bowl, whisk together the mustard, horseradish, and 1 tbsp. of olive oil until well-blended and brush all over filets.

5. Take trimmed asparagus and coat it with the remaining olive oil and lightly season with sea salt and black pepper, to taste.

6. Cut (8) 12 x 12-inch pieces of aluminum foil and double them up so that you are left with 4 pieces of double-thickness foil. Place one salmon filet and equal amounts of asparagus along each side of the salmon then fold and seal.

7. Place the four foil-wrapped filets on the grill and cook, grill lid closed, for about 15 minutes or until the asparagus is tender-crisp and the salmon flakes easily. Remove the foil and place onto 4 serving dishes.

Barbecued Sirloin in Dijon Dressing

For a flavorful dinner, try this sizzling, juicy grilled sirloin steak marinated in a creamy Dijon marinade that aids in the tenderness of the steak. Try serving alongside grilled mixed vegetables.

Yield: 4 (6-8 oz.) Sirloin Steaks; 1 c. Dijon Dressing
Servings: 2 (Serving Size: 1 (8 oz.) Sirloin Steaks; ¼ c. Dijon Dressing)
Total Time – Prep to Finish: 1 hour 30 minutes

Ingredients:

- 4 (6-8 oz.) beef sirloin steaks
- 2 tbsp. fresh basil, coarsely chopped
- 2 tbsp. ground black pepper
- 1 tbsp. Dijon mustard
- 1 tbsp. extra-virgin olive oil
- 2 tbsp. white wine vinegar

Directions:

1. In a bowl, combine the basil, the black pepper, the olive oil, the Dijon mustard and the white wine vinegar.

2. Rub the marinade onto the sirloin and refrigerate for 1½ hours.

3. Preheat the BBQ or grill to medium-high, and cook the sirloin 12 to 15 minutes on each side.

4. Let the meat rest around 15 minutes before serving.

Grilled Pork Chops with Sesame Slaw

Succulent, hearty, healthy, and delicious – that pretty much describes this dish. Lightly seasoned bone-in pork chops grilled to a golden excellence and served with a sesame slaw made of green cabbage and fresh cilantro and tossed in a dressing combining sesame seeds, orange juice, honey, and olive oil. Enjoy!

Yield: 4 (6 oz.) pork chops; 6 cups slaw
Servings: 4 (Serving Size: 1 (6 oz.) pork chop; 1½ c. slaw)
Total Time – Prep to Finish: 30 minutes

Ingredients:

- 4 (6 oz. each) bone-in pork chops
- 1¾ tsp. salt, divided
- 2 tsp. fresh ground black pepper, divided
- ¼ c. freshly-squeezed orange juice
- 2 tbsp. extra-virgin olive oil
- 2 tbsp. rice vinegar
- 2 tbsp. sesame seeds
- 1 tbsp. honey
- 1 small head Napa or green cabbage, thinly sliced (to yield 6 cups)
- 1 c. fresh cilantro leaves, chopped

Directions:

1. Preheat the grill to medium-high heat. Season each pork chop with about ¼ tsp. salt and ½ tsp. black pepper, or to taste. Cook the pork chops on the grill for about 6-7 minutes per side or until the chops are cooked through.

2. In a large salad bowl, combine the orange juice, olive oil, rice vinegar, sesame seeds, honey, and ¾ tsp. salt. Whisk until well combined, then add in the sliced cabbage and chopped cilantro and toss to combine. Place one pork chop on each plate alongside 1½ cups of the slaw. Serve and enjoy!

Chargrilled Chicken with Tropical Fruit

Enjoy the mouthwatering experience of perfectly chargrilled moist and tender chicken breasts served alongside sweet, juicy tropical mixed fruit such as papaya, star fruit, kiwi, and pineapple, in this Asian inspired dish.

Yield: 4 (4-6 oz.) boneless chicken breasts; 6-8 c. of frit
Servings: 1 (Serving Size: 4 (4-6 oz.) boneless chicken breast)
Total Time – Prep to Finish: 55 minutes

Ingredients:

- 4 (4-6 oz.) boneless chicken breasts, skin on
- Zest from 1 lime
- Juice from 5 limes
- 2 tbsp. extra-virgin olive oil
- 3-4 cloves garlic, crushed (to yield 2 tbsp. crushed)
- 2 kiwi fruit, peeled, sliced
- 1 small papaya, peeled, thinly sliced
- 1 star fruit, sliced
- 2 c. fresh pineapple, cut into small chunks

Directions:

1. Rinse the chicken breasts in cool water and pat dry with paper towels. Prepare the marinade by combining the lime zest, olive oil, and the 2 tbsp. of crushed garlic into a glass bowl. Whisk until the contents are well incorporated, then add in the chicken breasts, cover the bowl with plastic wrap, and place the bowl of chicken in the refrigerator for 30 minutes to marinate.

2. Meanwhile, prepare the fruit as directed above.

3. Preheat the grill. Grill the chicken breasts for about 4-5 minutes per side or until nicely charred and cooked through. The chicken should reach an internal temperature of 165°F. Remove the chicken from the grill and transfer each breast to a serving plate.

4. To serve, squeeze a little lime juice over each breast and top each chicken breast with one-fourth of the prepared tropical fruit (or serve the chicken alongside the fruit).

Pork Satay Kabobs

Spicy Thai dinner ideal for a summer evening get-togethers for backyard barbecues. Moist, tender pork is seasoned in a mixture of fresh cilantro, ginger, roasted red pepper, garlic, turmeric, cumin and more and then skewered and grilled until golden.

Yield: 16 kabobs
Servings: 4 (Serving Size: 3-4 kabobs)
Total Time – Prep to Finish: 45 minutes

Ingredients:

- 2-lbs. fresh pork meat, cut into chunks
- 3 c. coconut aminos
- 1 c. fresh cilantro, chopped fine
- ½ c. fresh ginger, shredded
- 4 roasted red peppers, chopped fine
- 8-12 cloves of garlic, chopped fine (amount dependent upon preferred taste)
- 2 2/3 tbsp. turmeric
- 2 2/3 tbsp. ground cumin
- ½ c. sesame oil
- 16 bamboo skewers, pre-soaked for 30 minutes in cool water

Directions:

1. In a large mixing bowl combine the soy sauce, cilantro, ginger, red pepper, 4-6 cloves chopped garlic (depending on personal preference), turmeric, cumin, and sesame oil and stir well to blend completely. Add in the pork pieces and let marinate in the refrigerator for at least 30 minutes.

2. Remove the marinated pork from the refrigerator and begin threading the pork pieces on to the skewers, try to get at least 4 pieces of pork onto each skewer, more if possible. For a twist, try threading on some fresh pineapple, bell pepper, mushrooms, etc.

3. When ready to cook, spray the grill grates with high-temperature cooking spray and preheat grill to medium-high heat. Place the skewers on the grill and cook approximately 3 to 5 minutes per side, turning as needed, until the pork is cooked through. Remove from grill and serve immediately.

Carne Asada with Mojo Marinade

In Mexico, Carne Asada is a very popular "street food" for social events. In America, it has found its way into our homes and hearts. Carne Asada is a dish known to bring people together – and that, in itself, is worthy of celebration. Juicy, succulent flank steak strips marinated in a sweet mojo sauce then grilled to perfection and served next to a flavorful side of Pico De Gallo. What's not to celebrate?

Yield: 16 oz. Carne Asada; ½-1 c. Pico De Gallo
Servings: 4 (Serving Size: (4 oz. Carne Asada; 2 tbsp. Pico De Gallo)
Total Time – Prep to Finish: 55 minutes

Ingredients:
For the Carne Asada:

- 1-lb. (16 oz.) Flank or Skirt steak
- Extra-virgin olive oil (to coat grill)
- Kosher salt, to taste
- Fresh ground black pepper, to taste

For the Mojo Marinade:

- 2 garlic clove, minced
- 1 jalapeno, seeded and minced
- 2 tbsp. fresh cilantro, chopped
- 1-2 limes, juiced (more/less to taste)
- 1½ tsp. white vinegar
- ¼-½ orange, juiced (more/less for preferred taste)
- 2 tbsp. extra-virgin olive oil
- Pinch kosher salt, or to taste
- Fresh ground black pepper, to taste

For the Pico De Gallo:

- 1 vine-ripened tomato, chopped (½ c.)
- 1 medium red onion, chopped (½ c.)
- 2 green onions, both parts sliced
- ½ Serrano chile pepper, minced
- 2 tbsp. fresh cilantro, chopped
- ½ tsp. garlic, minced
- ½-1 lime, juiced (more/less to taste)
- 3 tsp. extra-virgin olive oil
- Pinch kosher salt, or to taste

Directions:
1. Prepare the Mojo Marinade: In a food processor or mortar and pestle, mash together the garlic, jalapeno, cilantro, salt, and pepper. Blend the ingredients together to form a paste. Put the paste in a jar or container with a lid. Then add to the paste, the lime and orange

juices, white vinegar, and the olive oil. Seal the container and shake well to thoroughly blend the contents.

2. Prepare the Carne Asada: Lay the flank (or skirt) steak in a baking dish. Sprinkle steak with a pinch of salt and pepper. Pour the mojo marinade over the steak and rub it around to coat the surface of the steak. Cover with plastic wrap and let marinate for 15 minutes in the refrigerator. As soon as you place the steak in the refrigerator, prepare the Pico De Gallo.

3. Prepare the Pico De Gallo: In a medium-sized bowl, combine the tomato, red onion, green onion, Serrano chile, cilantro, minced garlic, lime juice, olive oil, and a pinch of salt. Mix the ingredients thoroughly. Let the Pico De Gallo rest in bowl at room temperature for 15 minutes to allow time for the flavors to meld.

4. Remove the steak from the refrigerator and let sit out next to the Pico De Gallo. Let the steak marinate for another 15 minutes at room temperature.

5. Preheat grill to medium-high heat. Coat the grates with olive oil to prevent sticking. Remove the steak from the mojo marinade and season both sides with a pinch of salt and pepper. Lay on the grill and cook the steak for about 7-10 minutes per side, turning only once, until the steak is medium-rare or preferred doneness is reached. Transfer steak to cutting board and let rest for about 5 minutes before slicing to allow the juices to settle within the steak. Then thinly slice the steak diagonally across the grain.

6. To serve, lay 4 ounces of Carne Asada onto each serving dish and top the Carne Asada with 2 tbsp. Pico De Gallo. Enjoy!

Kiwi Fruit Lamb Kabobs

Lamb is the perfect grilling meat – it is very hard to mess up and it always results in a meat that is tender and succulent. For this recipe, we took lamb meat, from either the leg or shoulder, marinated it in a sweet kiwi marinade, and then threaded it onto skewers and grilling it until golden.

Yield: 12 kabobs
Servings: 4 (Serving Size: 3 kabobs)
Total Time – Prep to Finish: 30 minutes

Ingredients:

- 1½-lbs. lamb meat (from leg or shoulder, cut into 1½-inch cubes
- 1 kiwi fruit
- 2 clove garlic, crushed
- 2 tbsp. coconut aminos
- 2 tbsp. dry sherry
- 1 tbsp. extra-virgin olive oil
- ½ tbsp. coconut palm sugar
- Pinch of fresh ground black pepper, or to taste

Directions:

1. First, if using bamboo/wooden skewers, be sure to pre-soak the skewers for at least 20 minutes to prevent burning during grilling.

2. Begin, by scooping the flesh out of the kiwi fruit and place it in a medium-sized bowl; using a fork, mash the kiwi very well. Stir in the crushed garlic, soy sauce, dry sherry, olive oil, white sugar, and black pepper. Blend until sugar is dissolved and contents are well incorporated.

3. Add in the lamb pieces and stir to coat well with the kiwi marinade. Cover bowl with lid or plastic wrap and marinate at room temperature for 20 minutes.

4. Using a slotted spoon, transfer the lamb from the bowl of kiwi marinade to a plate. Thread the lamb onto the bamboo skewers.

5. Preheat grill to high heat and barbecue the skewers for 5-7 minutes (turning the lamb from time to time) or until the lamb is cooked through and nicely browned on all sides – take care to not overcook the lamb, it can happen quickly. Divide the lamb kabobs among the 4 serving plates and serve alongside pineapple, white rice, or a veggie side dish.

Grilled Shrimp Skewers

A basic grilled shrimp skewer that turns out perfectly every time. Marinated in lemon, olive oil, fresh oregano, sage, chives, salt, and black pepper. Easy to make and goldenly delicious. Perfect for serving alongside a surf n' turf dish with shrimp and steak.

Yield: 12 skewers
Servings: 4 (Serving Size: 3 skewers)
Total Time – Prep to Finish: 45 minutes

Ingredients:

- 1 tsp. lemon zest, finely grated
- 1/3 c. fresh-squeezed lemon juice
- 3 tbsp. extra-virgin olive oil
- 2 tbsp. packed fresh oregano, minced
- 2 tbsp. packed fresh sage, minced
- 2 tbsp. minced fresh chives
- 1 tsp. fresh ground black pepper, or to taste
- ½ tsp. salt, or to taste
- 36 large or extra-large raw shrimp, peeled and deveined
- 12 bamboo skewers, soaked in water for 30 minutes

Directions:

1. Combine lemon zest, lemon juice, oil, oregano, sage, chives, pepper and salt in a large bowl. Reserve 2 tbsp. of the marinade.

2. Place the shrimp in the marinade and place in the refrigerator to marinate for 15 minutes.

3. Preheat grill to medium-high or place a grill pan over medium-high heat until hot.

4. Thread 3 shrimp onto each of the 12 skewers.

5. Oil the grill grates. Grill the shrimp until pink and firm, turning once, about 4 minutes total. Serve the shrimp skewers, drizzled with the reserved marinade.

Moroccan Spiced Grilled Chicken Breast

Tender and succulent chicken breast soaked in a creamy and flavorful marinade including plain yogurt, cilantro, paprika, and garlic. This is a recipe that the whole family will celebrate. Note: Chicken needs to be marinated in fridge for at least 6 hours.

Yield: 4 (4-6 oz.) grilled chicken breasts
Servings: 4 (Serving Size: 1 (4-6 oz.) grilled chicken breast)
Total Time – Prep to Finish: 6 hours 40 minutes

Ingredients:

- ½ c. dairy-free coconut yogurt, plain (Recommended: So Delicious brand)
- ½ c. fresh cilantro, chopped (or 1/3 tsp. ground coriander)
- ½ tbsp. extra-virgin olive oil
- 2 cloves garlic, minced
- 2/3 tsp. paprika
- 2/3 tsp. ground cumin
- ½ tsp. sea salt
- ½ tsp. fresh ground black pepper
- 4 (4-6 oz.) boneless, skinless chicken breasts

Directions:

1. In a medium-size bowl, mix together the yogurt, cilantro, olive oil, garlic, paprika, cumin, salt and pepper. Blend well.

2. Place chicken in a sealable, plastic freezer bag. Pour marinade over chicken. Seal bag and massage bag with hands to coat chicken with marinade. Place bag in a bowl and then place the chicken in the refrigerator for at least 6 hours, but no longer than overnight.

3. Prepare grill, by heating on high-heat. Grill chicken for 3-4 minutes on each side. Turning as needed until cooked through. Take care not to overcook.

4. To serve, transfer chicken to serving plate and serve hot.

Grilled Salmon with Tomatoes & Basil

Flaky, crispy grilled salmon topped with sliced tomato and fresh basil and then grilled in foil until done. Try serving alongside a cucumber salad or grilled zucchini.

Yield: 1 to 2-lb. salmon fillet
Servings: 4 (Serving Size: 1 (4-6 oz.) salmon fillet)
Total Time – Prep to Finish: 20 minutes

Ingredients:
- 2 cloves garlic, minced and smashed
- 1 tsp. kosher salt, divided
- 1 tbsp. extra-virgin olive oil
- 1 whole wild salmon fillet, cut into 4 (4-6 oz.) fillets
- 1/3 c. plus ¼ c. fresh basil, thinly sliced
- 2 medium tomatoes, thinly sliced
- ¼ tsp. fresh ground pepper, or to taste

Directions:
1. Preheat grill to medium.
2. Mash minced garlic and 3/4 tsp. of salt on a cutting board; using the side of a chef's knife , mash the minced garlic until a paste forms. Transfer the garlic paste to a small bowl; stir in the olive oil.
3. Check the salmon for pin bones and remove if necessary. Measure out a piece of heavy-duty foil (or use a double layer of regular foil) large enough for the salmon fillet. Coat the foil with cooking spray. Place the salmon skin-side down on the foil and spread the garlic mixture all over it. Sprinkle with 1/3 c. basil. Overlap tomato slices on top and sprinkle with the remaining ¼ tsp. salt and pepper.
4. Transfer the salmon on the foil to the grill. Grill until the fish flakes easily, 10 to 12 minutes. Use two large spatulas to slide the salmon from the foil to a serving platter. Cut into 4 equal portions and serve the salmon fillets sprinkled with the remaining ¼ c. basil.

Lamb Burgers with Mango Chutney

A wonderful and filling dish of juicy, succulent ground lamb burgers served on a bed of crisp lettuce leaves then topped with a flavorful mango chutney and a slice of crunchy red onion.

Yield: 4 burgers; 2 cups chutney
Servings: 2 (Serving Size: 1 burger; ½ c. chutney)
Total Time – Prep to Finish: 20 minutes

Ingredients:

- 1 to 1½-lbs. ground lamb.
- 1 large red onion, cut into 4 (¼-inch thick) rounds
- 1/3 c. red onion, chopped
- ½ c. mango chutney
- 1/8 tsp. salt, or to taste
- 4 large iceberg or Bibb lettuce leaves

Directions:

1. Preheat grill to medium-high.

2. Finely chop enough of one of the red onions to equal 50g. In a mixing bowl, combine the chopped onion, the lamb mince, 1 tbsp. chutney, and the salt. Gently mix with your hands until well combined. Form into 4 burgers, about 13 mm thick.

3. Coat the grill grates with high-heat cooking spray and grill the 4 red onion rounds for 3-4 minutes per side or until softened and charred in spots. Grill the lamb burgers for about 4-5 minutes per side or until cooked through.

4. Place 1 lamb burger onto each serving plate. Serve the chutney on the top of or alongside of the burger. Top each burger with one slice of grilled onion and 1 leaf of lettuce, if desired. Serve immediately.

Grilled Pork Chops with Peach Barbecue Sauce

A tangy, sweet peach-infused barbecue sauce is drizzled over perfectly grilled pork for an explosion of flavors. The sauce helps to keep the pork moist and tender during the grilling process. Try serving alongside a baby spinach salad.

Yield: 4 (4-6 oz.) pork chops
Servings: 4 (Serving Size: 1 pork chop)
Total Time – Prep to Finish: 1 hour 15 minutes

Ingredients:

- ¼ c. plus ½ tsp. kosher salt, divided
- ¼ c. maple syrup
- 2 c. boiling water
- 3 c. ice cubes
- 4 (4-6 oz.) bone-in, center-cut pork chops, trimmed
- 2 ripe, firm peaches, pitted/quartered (or 3 c. frozen sliced peaches)
- 1 medium tomato, quartered and seeded
- 2 tbsp. apple cider vinegar
- 1 tbsp. extra-virgin olive oil
- ½ c. onion, chopped
- 2 tsp. fresh ginger, chopped fine
- 2 tbsp. honey
- ¼ tsp. fresh ground black pepper, or to taste

Directions:

1. Place ¼ c. salt and the maple syrup in a medium-sized heat-proof bowl. Pour in boiling water and stir until dissolved. Add ice cubes; stir to cool. Add the pork chops, cover and refrigerate for at least 30 minutes.

2. In a blender or food processor, combine the peaches, tomato, and vinegar; purée until smooth.

3. 30 minutes prior to grilling the pork chops, heat the olive oil in a medium-sized saucepan over medium-high heat. Add in the onion and sauté, stirring occasionally, for about 5 minutes or until golden brown. Add in the ginger and cook, stirring frequently, for 1-2 minutes or until fragrant.

4. Pour in the peach purée, the remaining ½ tsp. salt, honey, and black pepper (to taste). Bring contents to a boil over high heat, then reduce heat to a simmer and let cook 20-25 minutes or until the sauce is reduced by nearly one-half. Reserve ¼ c. of the remaining sauce for basting the pork chops during grilling; keep the remaining sauce warm in the saucepan until ready to serve.

5. Preheat grill to medium.

6. Thoroughly rinse the pork chops in cold running water; pat dry using paper towels. Season the pork chops with ¼ tsp. black pepper and brush both sides with some of the reserved sauce.

7. Grill the pork chops for 2-4 minutes per side, turning only once, until an internal temperature

reaches 145°F. Transfer the pork chops to a plate, tent with foil, and let rest for 5 minutes.

8. To serve, place 1 pork chop on each plate alongside some of the peach barbecue sauce.

Beef-Veggie Kabobs with Honey Marinade

Tender top-sirloin marinated in a savory honey marinade and threaded onto bamboo skewers aside flavorful and juicy vegetables, then grilled to perfection. A fun and easy way to eat a delicious meal that everyone will love.

Yield: 12 beef kabobs
Servings: 4 (Serving Size: 3 beef kabobs)
Total Time – Prep to Finish: 1 hour 30 minutes

Ingredients:
For the Beef-Veggie Kabobs:
- 1-lb. top sirloin steak, cut in 1½-inch cubes
- 1 large green bell pepper
- 1-2 medium red onion
- 1-2 c. button mushrooms
- 24 bamboo or wooden skewers

For the Honey Marinade:
- 3 tbsp. extra-virgin olive oil
- 3 tbsp. coconut aminos
- 1½ tbsp. red wine vinegar
- 2-3 tbsp. honey
- 2 cloves garlic, minced
- 1 tbsp. fresh ginger, minced
- Pinch fresh ground black pepper, or to taste

Directions:
1. Prepare skewers by soaking in cool water for at least 30 minutes prior to grilling to prevent skewers from burning up on grill.
2. Prepare the Honey Marinade: In a gallon-size sealable Ziploc freezer bag, combine the olive oil, soy sauce, vinegar, honey, garlic, ginger, and a pinch of black pepper.
3. Prepare the Beef-Veggie Kabobs: Prepare the meat as directed and then add it to the bag of marinade. Seal the bag; shake/massage the outside of the bag to coat the meat well. Place the meat in the refrigerator to marinate for at least 30 minutes. Note: the longer you allow the meat to marinate, the more saturated the meat will become – marinating the meat overnight is ideal if time allows). If you are concerned about the possibility of the bag leaking inside the refrigerator, you can double-up the bag or you can place the bag of marinating meat in a large bowl and place it in the fridge that way.
4. Cut the bell pepper and onion into chunks about the width of the meat cuts. The mushrooms can be halved. Carefully, thread the beef and veggies on to double bamboo or wooden skewers in any pattern preferred, leaving a tiny space between pieces so that the kebabs grill more evenly. Using 2 skewers instead of 1 for each kebab will make the kebabs easier to turn on the grill. Drizzle any remaining marinade on to the kebabs or use the marinade to brush

the kabobs while on the grill. You should have a total of 12 kebabs.

5. Prepare grill for direct, high-heat. Spray the grates with high-heat cooking spray. Grill the kebabs for 8-10 minutes, turning occasionally, until meat is cooked to preferred doneness (internal temperature of 145°F for medium-rare).

6. Let kebabs rest for 5 minutes before serving. Serving size = 3 beef kebabs.

Citrus Grilled Chicken

A true summertime classic – boneless, skinless chicken breasts lightly seasoned with salt and black pepper, placed in an orange and lime marinade to soak, and then grilled to a golden finish. Fresh tropical fruit salads or rice pilafs are ideal accompaniments to this citrusy grilled chicken.

Yield: 4 (4-6 oz.) grilled chicken breasts
Servings: 4 (Serving Size: 1 (4-6 oz.)grilled chicken breast)
Total Time – Prep to Finish: 40 minutes

Ingredients:

- Zest of 2 oranges,, finely grated
- Juice of 2 oranges
- 2 limes
- 4 tbsp. extra-virgin olive oil
- 2 tsp. garlic, minced
- 4 (4-6 oz.) boneless, skinless chicken breasts
- ½ tsp. kosher salt, or to taste
- ½ tsp. black pepper, or to taste

Directions:

1. Place the orange zest and lime into a large-sized mixing bowl; mix well. Drizzle orange juice into the bowl; mix well. Add in olive oil and garlic; mix well.

2. Place chicken in marinade and toss to coat. Cover and let chicken marinate in the refrigerator for 15 minutes.

3. Place grill on medium-high heat. Spray grates with high heat cooking spray. Remove chicken from marinade, sprinkle with salt and pepper, and place on preheated grill. Grill chicken, turning occasionally, for 5 - 7 minutes per side or until chicken is turned juices run clear.

Mango & Lime BBQ Turkey

If you have yet to experience grilled turkey breast, you are in for quite a wonderful treat! This grilled turkey recipe results in slightly sweet, moist, and golden-grilled turkey breasts that go from grill to table in a matter of minutes.

Yield: 4 (6 oz.) grilled turkey breasts
Servings: 4 (Serving Size:
Total Time – Prep to Finish: 15 minutes

Ingredients:

- 4 (6 oz.) boneless, skinless turkey breasts
- Juice of 2 limes
- Zest of 2 limes
- Pinch fresh ground black pepper, or to taste
- 2 mangos, chopped
- High-heat cooking spray

Directions:

1. Combine the lime juice, lime zest, and black pepper in a sealable Ziploc bag. Add in the turkey, seal bag, and toss to coat.

2. Preheat grill to medium high and spray grates with a high heat cooking spray. Grill turkey for 5 to 7 minutes each side or until an internal temperature of about 165°F is reached.

3. While the turkey is grilling, chop up mango.

4. Remove turkey from grill and place on a serving dish. Top turkey breast with chopped mango, to garnish. Drizzle with a little lime juice, if preferred. Serve and enjoy!

Grilled Spiced Steak with Grilled Tomatoes

Tender sirloin steaks, seasoned with a mixture of garlic, coriander, cumin, and chili powder and then grilled and served alongside ripe, juicy tomatoes. You can also chop up the grilled tomatoes, add in some chopped grilled onion and top your steak with the chopped grilled veggies.

Yield: 4 (about 6 oz.) grilled sirloin streaks; 4 grilled tomatoes (8 halves)
Servings: 4 (Serving Size: 1 (6 oz.) grilled sirloin streak; 2 grilled tomato halves)
Total Time – Prep to Finish: 15 minutes

Ingredients:

- 4 (6 oz.) sirloin steaks (New York cut), all visible fat trimmed
- 2 tsp. extra-virgin olive oil
- 1 large garlic clove, crushed
- 1 tsp. water
- 1 tsp. ground coriander
- ½ tsp. ground cumin
- ¼ tsp. chili powder
- 4 ripe large tomatoes, halved lengthways

Directions:

1. Use a sharp knife to very lightly score both sides of the steak in a diamond pattern.

2. Combine the oil with the garlic, water, coriander, cumin and chili powder in a small bowl and mix well. Use a pastry brush to brush the mixture evenly over both sides of the steaks. Place on a plate, covered, in the fridge for 15 minutes to marinate.

3. Preheat a barbecue grill on medium-high.

4. Cook tomatoes on barbecue grill for 2-3 minutes each side or until browned on edges. Cook steaks for 4 minutes each side for medium-rare or until cooked to your liking.

5. Roughly chop tomatoes.

6. Serve steak with grilled tomatoes.

Pineapple & Grilled Chicken Stir-Fry

Simple and delicious and ready in under 20 minutes. A fulfilling, nutritious, protein- and vitamin C-packed meal that the whole family will love! Try serving over a bed of steamy hot rice!

Yield: 8 cups stir-fry
Servings: 4 (Serving Size: 2 cups stir-fry)
Total Time – Prep to Finish: 15 minutes

Ingredients:

- 2-lbs. boneless, skinless chicken breast; grilled then cut into chunks.
- 1 - 2 can(s) pineapple chunks, packed in pineapple juice (not syrup)
- 2 cloves garlic, minced
- ½-1 tbsp. fresh ginger root, minced
- 2 tbsp. extra virgin olive oil
- ½ green bell pepper, cut into strips or chunks
- ½ red bell pepper, cut into strips or chunks
- ½ onion, sliced or cut into chunks
- 3 scallions, sliced
- 3 c. broccoli (opt.)
- ½ c. pineapple juice (reserved from cans of pineapple chunks)
- 4 tbsp. coconut oil
- 1 tbsp. sesame oil (or extra-virgin olive oil, if preferred)
- 1½ tsp. arrowroot starch
- ½ -1 tbsp. honey
- 1 tbsp. coconut palm sugar (opt,)

Directions:

1. Preheat the grill to medium-high heat.

2. Prepare the Grilled Chicken: Lightly season the chicken breasts with salt and pepper and place on the grill. Grill the breasts for 5-7 minutes per side or until cooked through and juices run clear. Remove from grill and let rest at room temperature until the chicken is cool enough to handle. Then transfer the grilled chicken to a cutting board. Cut each breast into strips and then cut each strip into bite-size (approx. 1½-inch) chunks.

3. Prepare the Stir-Fry: Begin by draining the pineapple chunks, reserving ¼ c. of the pineapple juice for the sauce. Heat the olive oil in a large wok over medium heat. Add the grilled chicken pieces, minced garlic, and the minced ginger root. Stir-fry for 2 minutes. Add the pineapple chunks, onion, red and green pepper, and broccoli. Cover the wok and allow the contents to steam for about 2 to 3 minutes or until tender-crisp.

4. Prepare the Sauce: In a small bowl combine the reserved pineapple juice, coconut oil, sesame oil, arrowroot starch, honey, and coconut palm sugar (opt.) and whisk together until well blended. Drizzle the sauce over the contents in the wok. Add the scallions. Toss until the contents are coated with the sauce and the sauce begins to thicken.

5. Divide the stir-fry among two dinner plates and serve immediately.

Grilled Salmon & Lemon Skewers

These delightful grilled salmon and lemon kabobs are delectable and so simple to make – plus they offer up a heart healthy dose of Omega 3 fish oil in every unforgettably tasty bite. Try these kabobs for an fun and effortless way to introduce seafood to the kids. This light and flavorful fare is an excellent choice for any meal.

Yield: 8 skewers
Servings: 4 (Serving Size: 2 skewers)
Total Time – Prep to Finish: 15 minutes

Ingredients:

- 2 tbsp. fresh oregano, chopped
- 2 tsp. sesame seeds
- 1 tsp. ground cumin
- ¼ tsp. crushed red pepper flakes
- 1½-lbs. skinless wild salmon fillet, cut into 1-inch pieces
- 2 lemons, sliced into very thin rounds
- olive oil cooking spray
- 1 tsp. kosher salt
- 8 bamboo skewers soaked in water 1 hour

Directions:

1. First, preheat grill to medium and spray grates with a high heat cooking spray.

2. In a medium-sized mixing bowl, combine oregano, sesame seeds, cumin, and red pepper flakes and mix well; set aside.

3. Begin threading the bamboo skewers: Start by taking a piece of salmon and threading it onto two side-by-side skewers (using two skewers instead of one will make the kabobs sturdier throughout the grilling and handling process). Next, fold one of the lemon rounds and thread it onto the same skewers. Alternate salmon and lemon until 8 total kabobs have been threaded. Make sure that each kabob begins and ends with a piece of salmon.

4. Lightly spray each kabob with olive oil cooking spray. Next, sprinkle each kabob with a pinch of salt and then season the kabobs with the spice-mixture.

5. Place kabobs on grill and cook for approximately 8 to 10 minutes (turning the kabobs occasionally) or until salmon is cooked through and flakes easily. Place 2 kabobs onto each serving dish and serve immediately.

Grilled Herb-Crusted Ribeye & Grilled Pineapple

Flavorful, tender, cooked-to-order ribeye steak which have been delicately rubbed with a mixture of herbs and seasonings. The grilled pineapple is brushed with a honey-cinnamon marinade and helps bring sweetness to this dish that only pineapple can.

Yield: 4 (6 to 8 oz.) ribeye steaks and 8-10 slices pineapple
Servings: 4 (Serving Size: 1 (6 to 8 oz.) ribeye steak and 2 slices pineapple)
Total Time – Prep to Finish: 45 minutes

Ingredients:
For the Herb-Crusted Ribeye:

- 4 (6-8 oz.) ribeye steaks
- 4 tbsp. dried basil
- 4 tsp. dried thyme
- 2 tbsp. fresh rosemary chopped
- 4 tsp. dried oregano
- 2 tbsp. crushed fennel seeds
- 2 tsp. ground coriander
- 4 tsp garlic powder
- 2 tbsp. sea salt
- 4 tsp. fresh ground black pepper

For the Pineapple:

- 1 (2-lb.) fresh pineapple, peeled/sliced (½-inch thick)
- 2 tbsp. lime juice
- 2 tbsp. lemon juice
- 4 tbsp. honey
- 1 tsp. cinnamon

Directions:

1. Let the steaks rest at room temperature for 30 minutes.

2. Preheat the grill to high heat.

3. Prepare the Herb Crusted Steak: In a bowl, combine the basil, thyme, rosemary, oregano, fennel seeds, coriander, garlic powder, sea salt, and black pepper. Stir to combine. Set aside.

4. Prepare the Pineapple: In a separate bowl, combine the lime juice, lemon juice, honey, and cinnamon. Whisk until blended and the cinnamon is dissolved. Set aside.

5. Peel and cut the pineapple into slices/wedges/triangles (whichever shape preferred) that are ½-inch thick.

6. Generously brush both sides of the sliced pineapple with the honey-cinnamon marinade.

7. After the steak has sat at room temperature for 30 minutes, generously dry rub the steak

seasoning over both sides of each steak. Set aside.

8. Place the steaks and pineapple slices on the preheated grill. Cook the steaks for about 4-5 minutes per side for medium-well or until desired doneness is reached. Grill the pineapple for 4-5 minutes per side or until the pineapple is slightly softened and is left with nice grill marks.

9. Place each steak onto a serving dish alongside 2 wedges of pineapple and enjoy!

Grilled Jerk Chicken

In the mood for some fiery spicy chicken? This is a simple jerk chicken using a seasoning rub combining Scotch bonnet peppers, allspice, cinnamon, nutmeg, etc. – like in authentic Jamaican Jerk recipes – only were turning the flavor up a notch and adding a bit of molasses and dark rum. This recipe offers an explosion of amazing flavors you'll enjoy. Note: Allow enough time for chicken to marinate in refrigerator overnight prior to grilling.

Yield: 1-lb. chicken – 8 chicken thighs
Servings: 4 (Serving Size: 4 oz. cooked chicken – 2 chicken thighs))
Total Time – Prep to Finish: 35 minutes (Marinate in refrigerator overnight)

Ingredients:
- ¼ c. white vinegar
- 1¼ tbsp. dark rum (opt.)
- 2 Scotch bonnet peppers or habaneros, with seeds, chopped
- 1 red onion, chopped
- 2 green onion tops, chopped
- 2 tsp. dried thyme (or 1¼ tbsp. fresh thyme leaves, chopped)
- 1¼ tbsp. extra-virgin olive oil
- 1 tsp. salt
- 1 tsp. fresh ground black pepper
- 3 tsp. ground allspice
- 3 tsp. ground cinnamon
- 3 tsp. ground nutmeg
- 3 tsp. ground ginger
- 1 tsp. molasses
- (8) bone-in chicken thighs (1-lb.)
- ¼ c. lime juice
- Salt, to taste
- Fresh ground black pepper, to taste

Directions:

1. Combine vinegar, dark rum (opt.), chopped pepper, chopped red onion and chopped green onion tops, thyme, olive oil, 1 tsp. salt, 1 tsp. black pepper, allspice, cinnamon, nutmeg, ginger, and molasses into a blender. Pulse about 30 seconds or until completely smooth.

2. Place chicken thighs in a sealable plastic freezer bag, drizzle lime juice over the chicken and coat well. Pour the jerk paste into the plastic bag, seal bag and coat well, massaging paste into chicken with hands. Refrigerate chicken and allow it to marinate in the paste overnight.

3. Prepare to cook chicken. Remove chicken from plastic bag. Put the remaining marinade from bag into a small saucepan. Bring to a boil, reduce heat and let simmer for 10 minutes. Set aside to use as basting sauce.

4. Preheat grill to medium-high and sprinkle chicken thighs with salt and pepper to season.

Place chicken thighs onto grill grates. Cover grill with lid and grill chicken thighs slowly until cooked, turning and basting occasionally. The chicken is done with juices run clear and when an internal temperature of 180-185°F for thighs about 15-20 minutes.

5. Transfer chicken to serving plates and serve hot alongside desired salad or side dish.

Spicy Citrus Ribs with Spicy Honey-Maple Glaze

A quick and simple way to prepare mouth-watering ribs without the need for a smoker or hours of time waiting and watching. In a short time, you will have juicy, tender, and flavorful ribs that were first infused with a citrusy and spicy brine that will make the ribs plump and succulent and then brushed with a sweet honey-maple glaze that offers a kick of fiery spice. This is a pork ribs recipe that your friends will covet and your family will crave.

Yield: 1 to 1½-lbs. pork ribs – 8-12 individual ribs)
Servings: 4 (Serving Size: (4 oz. pork ribs – 2-3 individual ribs)
Total Time – Prep to Finish: 1 hour 25 minutes

Ingredients:
For the Ribs:
- 1 to 1½-lbs. full-rack of ribs
- 2½ c. spicy citrus brine (see recipe)
- Cooking spray for grill grates
- 1 c. spicy honey-maple glaze (see recipe)

For the Spicy Honey-Maple Glaze:
- ½ c. honey
- 2 tbsp. maple syrup
- 2 tsp. coconut palm sugar
- ¼ tsp. crushed red pepper flakes
- 1 tsp. salt, or to taste
- ½ tsp. fresh ground black pepper, to taste
- 1¼ tbsp. grass-fed butter

For the Spicy Citrus Brine:
- 2-3 oranges, juiced (to yield 11/3 c.)
- 2-3 lemons, juiced (to yield ½ c.)
- 2-3 limes, juiced (to yield ¼ c.)
- ½ c. water
- 16-20 mint leaves, chopped, plus some to garnish
- 1 tsp. dried thyme
- 1 tbsp. crushed red pepper flakes

Directions:
- Prepare the Spicy Citrus Brine: Combine the citrus juices and water into a measuring cup, you should have about 1¼ cups liquid then combined. If you have more or less, pour out or add more water to reach 1¼ cups. Pour the liquid into a medium-size bowl and add

97

salt, dried thyme, and red pepper. Stir for about 30 seconds until all salt has dissolved..

- Prepare the Ribs: If desired, remove the thin membrane that lines the concave of the rack. This will allow the marinade and glaze to penetrate deeper into the meat. Place rack in freezer bag and pour brine into the bag. Seal bag, squeezing out any excess air. Using hands, massage the brine into the ribs. Place the sealed bag of ribs into a bowl. Allow to marinate in refrigerator for 3-6 hours, NO longer.

- Prepare the Spicy Honey-Maple Glaze: Begin by beating the glaze ingredients together in a small saucepan over medium-low heat. Stir in red pepper flakes, black pepper, and salt. Whisk in the butter until melted..

- Prepare grill for indirect heat. On a gas grill heat to a temp of 300-325°F, leaving the middle burners turned off. For charcoal grill, use 2-3lbs, of briquettes, pushed off to one side. Set an aluminum drip pan next to briquettes, under where the ribs will be.

- Remove ribs from plastic bag and pat dry with paper towel. Coat grill grates with olive or canola oil. Place ribs on side of grill away from source of heat (gas/briquettes). Cover grill with lid, maintaining a heat of 300-325°F the entire time. If using charcoal grill, adjust vents so airflow is reduced. Grill for 20-25 minutes than flip ribs over. Cook for about 15-20 more minutes and then use meat thermometer to check for doneness. The ribs will be ready to pull of grill at a temp of 155°F. However, apply the glaze about 10 minutes before they are done - so at 145°F, start applying the glaze, turning and basting until all glaze is used. When the thickest part of the ribs read a temp of 155°F, pull ribs off the grill.

- Transfer to serving dish and serve hot!

GRILLED VEGETABLE RECIPES

Grilled Artichokes

Grilling is one of the tastiest ways to enjoy artichokes! This recipe for grilled artichokes involves a lemon-garlic marinade that adds just enough flavor to turn this into a go-to artichoke recipe for your family, because once you experience grilled artichokes like this you won't be able to imagine them any other way!

Yield: 8 quarters of grilled artichoke
Servings: 4 (Serving Size: 2 quarters of the grilled artichoke with dip)
Total Time – Prep to Finish: 2 hours 45 minutes (Includes 2 hours marinating time)

Ingredients:
- 4 large artichokes
- 2 lemons, halved
- ½ c. balsamic vinegar
- ½ c. extra-virgin olive oil
- 2 tbsp. fresh garlic, minced
- ¼ c. fresh parsley, finely chopped
- 1¼ tbsp. sea salt, or to taste, divided
- 2 tsp. fresh ground black pepper, or to taste
- 2 tsp. Dijon mustard, or as needed for dip (opt.)

Directions:
1. First, prepare the artichokes by cutting off the bottom stem and the pointy tips from each choke. Rub the cut ends with half a lemon to prevent browning.
2. Bring a Dutch oven or a large pot of water with 1 tsp. salt to a vigorous boil. Carefully lower in the trimmed artichokes. Make sure they stay submerged in the water (use a plate to weight them down, if needed). Cook for approximately 20 minutes or until the bottom of each choke is fork tender. Drain and set the chokes aside until they are cool enough to handle.
3. In a medium-sized mixing bowl, combine the balsamic vinegar, olive oil, minced garlic, chopped parsley, and salt and pepper, to taste. Whisk until completely blended.
4. Cut each artichoke into quarters, starting from the base of the choke and cutting downwards towards the tips of the leaves. Using a spoon, remove the fur and inner leaves. Place the chokes in the marinade and let marinate for at least 2 hours, up to 6 hours total.
5. Preheat the grill to medium-high. Place the marinated artichokes on the grill, cut-side-down, and grill for 2-3 minutes or until golden brown. Turn and cook for another 3 minutes; drizzle each with 1-2 tsp. of the marinade.
6. Add 1 tsp. Dijon mustard to the remaining marinade and whisk until a smooth dip results, adding additional mustard if needed.
7. Serve the artichokes with the dip.

Grilled Romaine with Toasted Almonds and Caesar Dressing

Perfectly grilled romaine lettuce drizzled In a creamy Caesar dressing and then sprinkled with lightly toasted almonds. Try serving by itself as a light lunch or alongside grilled meat or seafood.

Yield: 4 halves grilled romaine heads
Servings: 4 (Serving Size: 1 half grilled romaine head)
Total Time – Prep to Finish: 20 minutes

Ingredients:
For the Grilled Romaine:

- 2 Romaine Heads, cut in half
- ¼ c. almonds, toasted/coarsely chopped
- avocado oil for brushing (or preferred oil)

For the Mayonnaise:

- 2 egg yolks
- 1 tsp. mustard (opt.)
- 3 tsp. fresh-squeezed lemon juice
- ½ c. olive oil
- ½ c. coconut oil, melted
- Pinch of salt, or to taste (opt.)
- Pinch of black pepper, or to taste (opt.)

For the Caesar Dressing:

- 5 anchovy filets packed in olive oil, finely minced
- 2 tbsp. mayonnaise (see recipe)
- 1/3 c. extra-virgin olive oil
- 1 tbsp. Dijon mustard
- 1 tbsp. balsamic vinegar
- 3 cloves garlic, grated
- juice from ½ a lemon
- 1 tsp. salt , or to taste
- ½ tsp. fresh ground black pepper, or to taste

Directions:

1. Preheat grill to high heat.
2. Prepare the Mayonnaise: Place the egg yolks in a blender or food processor along with the mustard (if using) and 1 tsp. lemon juice. Pulse until well blended. With the motor still running, very slowly begin to add the olive oil, a drop or two at a time. Continue until the mixture emulsifies. The mayo will begin to thicken as it emulsifies. When both the olive oil

101

and the coconut oil is fully incorporated and the mayo is thick, add in the remaining lemon juice, and salt and pepper, to taste. Transfer to a bowl, cover with plastic wrap and place in the refrigerator until needed.

3. Prepare the Caesar Dressing: In a medium-sized mixing bowl, combine the Dijon mustard, balsamic vinegar, and grated garlic. Whisk to combine. Stir in the mayonnaise and whisk until thoroughly incorporated. Continue whisking, while gradually adding in the olive oil, drop by drop, until the dressing begins to thicken slightly and then continue adding it in a slow steady stream, whisking the entire time. Add in the anchovy filets and the lemon juice; whisk until thoroughly incorporated.

4. Prepare the Romaine: Preheat the grill to medium-high heat. Slice each romaine head in half and brush both sides with the avocado oil (or preferred oil). Place the romaine on the grates and grill for 2-4 minutes on each side, or until deep grill marks appear.

5. Place a small skillet over medium heat. Add in the almonds and toast, shaking the skillet often, for 3-5 minutes or until the almonds become fragrant and lightly browned. Transfer to a cutting board; chop coarsely.

6. To serve, place 1 half of a grilled romaine head onto each serving dish. Serve with the Caesar dressing and toasted almonds.

Grilled Vegetable Kabobs with Pesto

These delicious vegetable kabobs are made by combining eggplant, zucchini, bell pepper, cherry tomatoes, and red onions. They are then tossed with a flavorful pesto and then grilled to perfection. These kabobs are ideal when served alongside steak and chicken. Note: You can use any combination of vegetables, so these kabobs adapt wonderfully to the passing seasons!

Yield: 4 halves grilled romaine heads
Servings: 4 (Serving Size: 1 half grilled romaine head)
Total Time – Prep to Finish: 30 minutes

Ingredients:
For the Vegetable Kabobs:

- 2 eggplant, cut into chunks
- 2 zucchini, cut into chunks
- 3 bell peppers, cut into chunks
- 1 pint cherry tomatoes
- 2 red onions, cut into quarters
- 1/2 of the pesto sauce (or desired amount)
- 12 bamboo skewers (pre-soaked in water)

For the Pesto:

- 1½ c. fresh basil leaves, tightly packed
- 2 tbsp. fresh parsley, chopped
- 2 cloves garlic, roughly chopped
- ½ c. pine nuts
- Salt, to taste
- Fresh ground black pepper, to taste
- ½ c. extra-virgin olive oil

Directions:

1. Place the bamboo skewers in cool water to soak for 20 minutes.

2. Prepare the Pesto: Combine all of the ingredients, except for the olive oil, into a food processor or blender. Process until a smooth paste forms.

3. With the motor running, slowly drizzle in the oil until your desired consistency is reached. Adjust seasonings as needed.

4. Preheat the grill to medium-high heat.

5. Prepare the Vegetable Kabobs: Prepare the vegetables as directed and then place them in a large bowl. Pour half of the pesto (or desired amount) into the bowl over the vegetables and toss until the vegetables are completely coated.

6. Skewer the vegetables in desired order onto the pre-soaked skewers and grill for 5-7 minutes, turning as needed, until the veggies are lightly charred and fork tender.

7. Serve with the remaining pesto, if desired.

Grilled Acorn Squash

This grilled acorn squash recipe results in a delicious, wholesome, and filling side dish that goes perfectly with most any type of grilled meat, chicken, or fish.

Yield: 8 pieces of grilled acorn squash
Servings: 4 (Serving Size: 2 quarters of the grilled squash)
Total Time – Prep to Finish: 60 minutes

Ingredients:
- Juice of 1 orange
- 1 clove garlic, minced
- ½ tbsp. white balsamic vinegar (or white wine vinegar)
- ½ tbsp. fresh rosemary, chopped fine
- ¼ tsp. salt, or to taste
- 2 tbsp. extra-virgin olive oil
- 2 medium-large sized acorn squash, quartered, seeds/ fibers removed and discarded

Directions:
1. Place a small saucepan over medium heat. Add in the orange and bring to a boil. Let the juice continue to boil for 5-10 minutes or until it is reduced to about 2 tbsp. of liquid. Remove the saucepan from the heat and stir in the garlic, balsamic vinegar, rosemary, and salt. Whisk until fully incorporated. Next, whisk in the olive oil until contents are well combined.

2. Preheat grill to medium.

3. Wash the squash, cut each squash into quarters; remove and discard seeds and fibers. Place squash quarters on grill, peel-side-down. Brush the pieces of squash generously with the orange-rosemary glaze, close the grill lid, and cook for 40-50 minutes (brushing the squash every 10-15 minutes with the glaze) or until the squash is soft and the edges are nicely browned.

4. Place 2 pieces of grilled squash on each serving plate. This grilled squash goes perfectly with any grilled meat, chicken, or fish. Serve and enjoy!

Perfect Roasted Garlic on the Grill

Roasted garlic is delicious. Plain and simple. Preparing roasted garlic on the grill is a simple way to get it on your dinner table. Many people also eat roasted garlic whole, straight from the clove. When garlic is roasted, it becomes sweet tasting and really tastes just as great on its own as it does in a dish AND it don't worry, it doesn't affect your breath in the way raw garlic does! There are so many uses and possibilities for roasted garlic. So the next time you fire up the grill, throw on a few bulbs of garlic for a truly satisfying treat!

Yield: 4 bulbs of roasted garlic
Servings: 4 (Serving Size: 1 bulb of roasted garlic)
Total Time – Prep to Finish: 45 minutes

Ingredients:
- 4 heads garlic
- 4 tsp. extra-virgin olive oil
- sea salt, to taste

Directions:
1. Preheat the grill to medium-high and set up it up for indirect heat.

2. Using a sharp knife, cut off the top of each head of garlic. Double check to make sure the tips have been cut off of each of the individual cloves. (You want to be able to easily squeeze the garlic from the cloves).

3. Next, cut out 8 squares of aluminum foil. Double-up the squares so that you are left with 4 squares of double-layered foil. Place a head of garlic in the center of each square and drizzle each head of garlic with 1 tsp. olive oil. Then sprinkle a little sea salt onto each garlic bulb and wrap the bulbs up in the foil.

4. Place the foil-wrapped garlic on the preheated grill. Close the grill and roast the garlic bulbs for 30-45 minutes or until the garlic feels soft when squeezed.

5. Remove the garlic from the grill, unwrap and discard the foil, and serve as desired.

Grilled Asparagus

Firm asparagus spears are lightly drizzled in olive oil and seasoned with sea salt and then grilled until the natural sugars in the spears have caramelized giving off a spectacular flavor experience. Serve along side grilled steak, chicken, pork, salmon, or in any way you wish. Grilled asparagus is versatile and goes well with pretty much everything!

Yield: 1-lb. grilled asparagus
Servings: 4 (Serving Size: ¼-lb.)
Total Time – Prep to Finish: 15 minutes

Ingredients:

- 1-lb fresh asparagus, trimmed and peeled
- 4 tbsp. extra-virgin olive oil
- 1 tsp. sea salt, or to taste

Directions:

1. Preheat the grill to medium-high.

2. Place the asparagus spears on a plate, drizzle the oil over the asparagus and turn the spears in the oil to coat. Next, season with sea salt, turning the spears again to coat.

3. Place the spears on the preheated grill and grill for 5 minutes, rolling each spear by ¼ turn every minute. When the asparagus begins to brown in spots, remove from the grill. Do not allow the asparagus to char and control any flare-ups from the dripping oil with a spritz of water from a spray bottle.

4. Serve the grilled asparagus immediately.

GRILLED SNACKS & DESSERT RECIPES

Honey-Cinnamon Grilled Peaches

A delicious summertime treat! Ripe, velvety-sweet peaches are brushed with a honey-butter and cinnamon glaze and then placed on the grill until perfectly charred. They are then garnished with a dollop of whipped topping and a sprinkle of cinnamon!

Yield: 8 peach halves
Servings: 4 (Serving Size: 2 peach halves)
Total Time – Prep to Finish: 15 minutes

Ingredients:
- 4 ripe peaches, cut in half; pits removed and discarded
- 4 tbsp. coconut butter or ghee
- 4 tbsp. honey
- 4 tsp. cinnamon, plus more to garnish
- Dairy-free whipped topping, to garnish.

Directions:
1. Make sure grill grates are clean; preheat grill to high

2. Slice each peach in half; remove and discard pits.

3. Place a small saucepan over medium-low heat. Combine the coconut butter (or ghee), honey, and the cinnamon. Cook, stirring constantly, for 3-5 minutes or until the mixture is melted and smooth.

4. Brush the cut side of each peach with the honey-cinnamon mixture and place the peaches on the grill, cut-side-down. Brush the skin of the peaches with the remaining honey-cinnamon mixture. Close the grill lid and grill the peach halves for 3-4 minutes or until the peaches are perfectly charred and heated through.

5. Transfer 2 peach halves per serving dish. Top each with a dollop of dairy-free coconut cream whipped topping and a sprinkle of cinnamon, if desired. Serve warm.

Coconut Lime Sorbet with Grilled Strawberries

Here is an icy summertime treat that will cool you off and kill sugar cravings in a healthy way. Coconut-lime sorbet that is slightly sweetened to the perfect degree and then topped with plump, juicy grilled strawberries. Note: If you prefer lemons to limes, just switch the two out and continue to the follow recipe as if nothing changed.

Yield: 1 quart (4 cups) sorbet; 8 grilled strawberry skewers
Servings: 4 (Serving Size: 1 c. sorbet; 2 grilled strawberry skewers)
Total Time – Prep to Finish: 20 minutes

Ingredients:

- 2 (15 oz.) cans cream of coconut
- 1½ c. water
- 1 c. fresh-squeezed lime juice
- 24 medium-large size, ripe, fresh strawberries
- 1 c. fine coconut palm sugar
- 8 (6-inch) bamboo skewers (soaked in cool water for 30 minutes prior to use)
- ½ c. shredded unsweetened coconut, lightly toasted (opt.), to garnish
- ½ c. almonds, sliced and toasted (opt.), to garnish

Directions:

1. Prepare the sorbet: In a large mixing bowl, combine the cream of coconut, water, and fresh-squeezed lime juice. Whisk until thoroughly incorporated. Place the mixture in an ice cream maker and proceed by following manufacturer instructions. When finished, transfer the sorbet to an airtight container and store in the freezer until firm.

2. When the sorbet is ready to be served, begin preparing the strawberries.

3. Preheat grill to medium-low heat. Grease the grates with high heat cooking spray.

4. Thread 3 strawberries onto each of the 8 skewers leaving ¼-inch of space between each berry.

5. If using a coarser coconut palm sugar, place the sugar in a food processor and process until it is as fine as granulated sugar, then transfer the coconut palm sugar onto a shallow plate. Roll the skewered berries in the sugar, turning to evenly coat.

6. Place the skewered strawberries on the preheated grill and grill, covered, for 5-6 minutes, turning frequently, until the strawberries are evenly grilled.

7. To serve, place 1 c. of sorbet in a bowl, garnish with toasted coconut and sliced almonds, if desires. Serve with 2 grilled strawberry skewers.

Grilled Mango Blossom

Juicy, sweet mango halves are scored to resemble a flower blossom and are then grilled to a golden brown perfection and brushed with molasses. The blossoms are served over pureed kiwi and mango syrups. For a special treat, serve the mango blossoms alongside vanilla ice cream, if desired.

Yield: 6 mango blossoms
Servings: 6 (Serving Size: 1 mango blossom)
Total Time – Prep to Finish: 40 minutes

Ingredients:

- 3 mangoes
- 3 kiwifruit, peeled
- 2 tablespoons molasses

Directions:

- Place 6 dessert bowls in the freezer to chill.

- Prepare the mango by cutting each one in half lengthwise on either side (flat side) of the seed. Remove the seed portions and set them aside. Using a paring knife score the mango halves (CUTTING TO, BUT NOT THROUGH THE PEEL) in a crisscross pattern all the way across the mango. PEEL; set aside.

- Carefully remove and discard the peel from around the reserved mango seeds. Cut away as much of the fruit remaining around each seed as you can and then discard the seeds. Place the flesh of the fruit in a food processor or blender and purée until smooth. Transfer the pureed fruit to a clean plastic squeeze bottle and place in the refrigerator to chill.

- Clean out the food processor or blender and now place in the peeled kiwifruit. Purée until smooth, then transfer to a second plastic squeeze bottle and place in the refrigerator to chill.

- Preheat the grill to medium and grease the grates with cooking spray. Place the mango halves on the grill scored side down and grill for 4-6 minutes or until the edges are lightly browned and the mangos are heated through. During the last minute of grilling brush each mango with the molasses.

- Remove the puréed mango and kiwi squeeze bottles from the refrigerator and drizzle the purées into each of the six chilled dessert bowls. Gently bend the peel back from each half of the mangos. Push the inside up and out until the mango cubes pop up, separate, and "blossom." Place 1 mango blossom into each of the puréed dessert bowls. Serve immediately.

Honey Glazed Grilled Plums

Sweet, plump plums are coated in honey and grilled lightly, just until the plums are slightly browned and the juices have released and the peaches have softened slightly. The peaches are then served over vanilla-flavored frozen yogurt and drizzled in additional honey.

Yield: 4 grilled plums
Servings: 4 (Serving Size: 1 grilled plum, halved)
Total Time – Prep to Finish: 10 minutes

Ingredients:

- 4 (about ¾-lb.) firm, fresh plums, halved/pitted
- 10 tbsp. honey, divided
- 4 c. non-dairy vanilla-flavored frozen yogurt (or flavor of choice) (Recommended Brands: Silk, Cloud Top, Turtle Mountain, Julies Organic, Almond Dream, or you can fairly easily make your own at home!)

Directions:

1. Preheat the grill to medium heat. Grease the grates well with cooking spray or brush with olive oil.

2. Wash the plums in cool running water; pat dry using paper towels. Cut each plum in half; remove and discard the pits.

3. Place 6 tbsp. of the honey in a medium sized mixing bowl, add in the halved, pitted plums and toss to coat.

4. Place the plums on the grill and grill the plums, flesh side down, for 2-3 minutes or until lightly browned, then flip the plum halves and grill, this time skin-side-down, for 1-3 more minutes or until the plums are slightly softened and heated through.

5. To serve, place 1 c. frozen yogurt into each serving bowl and top each with 2 peach halves. And drizzle the dis with 1 tbsp. honey, if desired. Serve immediately.

Grilled Pineapple-Coconut Sundae

Juicy, grilled pineapple that is perfectly charred paired with icy frozen yogurt and flaky shredded and loghty toasted coconut for a summertime dessert experience that is monumental. Guests, kids, everyone will love this dessert – it tastes so good - and it is actually good for you!

Yield: 4 sundaes
Servings: 4 (Serving Size: 1 sundae)
Total Time – Prep to Finish: 30 minutes

Ingredients:

- ½ (2-lb.) pineapple, peeled/cored and sliced into rings ½-inch-thick
- 1-2 tsp. coconut oil, melted (or olive oil, if preferred)
- ½ c. shredded coconut
- 4 cups (1 quart) dairy-free vanilla-flavored vanilla frozen yogurt (or flavor of choice) (Recommended Brands: Silk, Cloud Top, Turtle Mountain, Julies Organic, Almond Dream, or you can fairly easily make your own at home!)
- Mint sprigs, for garnish

Directions:

1. Preheat the grill to medium-high heat.

2. Peel and core the pineapple and cut it into ½-inch thick rings.

3. Using a pastry brush both sides of the pineapple rings with the melted coconut oil (or olive oil).

4. Place the pineapple rings on the preheated grill and let the rings grill for 5-8 minutes, turning every so often until the pineapple is slightly softened and perfectly charred with marks from the grill grates. Transfer grilled pineapple rings to a cutting board. You can cut the rings in half, cut them into bite-size pieces or you can leave the rings whole.

5. Place a medium-sized skillet over medium-low, add in the shredded coconut and toast for about 2 minutes or until lightly golden. In a medium skillet, toast the coconut over moderate heat until golden, about 2 minutes. Remove from heat and set aside to cool.

6. When the coconut has cooled, scoop 1 c. of frozen yogurt into each sundae dish (or dessert bowls). Top the frozen yogurt with the grilled pineapple and then sprinkle the sundaes with the toasted coconut and mint sprigs, to garnish. Serve and enjoy immediately.

Grilled Honey-Mint Cantaloupe Skewers

Deliciously ripe cubes of cantaloupe coated in olive oil and grilled until lightly charred, they are then drizzled with golden sweet honey and sprinkled with sea salt and fresh minced mint. A sweet treat that can be served as an appetizer, side or dessert!

Yield: 8 cantaloupe skewers
Servings: 4 (Serving Size: 2 cantaloupe skewers)
Total Time – Prep to Finish: 15 minutes

Ingredients:

- 2 cantaloupes, peeled/seeded cut into 2-inch chunks
- 2 tbsp. extra virgin olive oil
- 2 tbsp. honey
- 2 tsp. minced fresh mint
- 2 tsp. sea salt
- 8 bamboo skewers (soaked in cool water for 30 minutes prior to using)

Directions:

1. Preheat grill to medium-high heat.

2. Peel, remove the seeds and cut the cantaloupe into 2-inch pieces.

3. Thread the cantaloupe onto the pre-soaked bamboo skewers.

4. Using a pastry brush, push the skewered cantaloupe with the olive oil so that all sides are coated well.

5. Place the cantaloupe on the grill and grill for 3-4 minutes or until lightly golden and slightly softened.

6. Transfer 2 skewers to each plate and drizzle the honey over the skewered cantaloupe, then sprinkle with the sea salt and minced fresh mint. Serve immediately.

Grilled Marinated Apples with Mint

Sweet, honey-orange-mint marinated apples grilled until just tender and perfectly charred. Enjoy them as a sweet treat by themselves or serve them as the perfect companion to grilled pork or chicken. Try using Red or Golden Delicious apples for the sweetest results or Granny Smith also works very well for a more tart, yet still sweet, taste!

Yield: 16 grilled apple slices
Servings: 4 (Serving Size: 4 grilled apple slices)
Total Time – Prep to Finish: 15 minutes

Ingredients:

- 1½ c. fresh-squeezed orange juice
- 2 tbsp. fresh mint, chopped fine
- ¼ c. honey
- 2 tsp. vanilla extract
- 1 tsp. ground ginger
- ½ tsp. fresh ground black pepper
- 4 Granny Smith or Red/Golden Delicious apples; cored & cut crosswise into 4 (½-inch-thick) slices
- Cooking spray

Directions:

1. In a gallon-size sealable Ziploc plastic bag, combine the orange juice, chopped mint, honey, vanilla extract, ginger, and black pepper. Seal the bag and shake and massage the bag to thoroughly blend the marinade.

2. Core the apples, leaving the peels intact; cut each apple into 4 (½-inch-thick) slices for a total of 16 slices.

3. Place the apple slices in the bag; seal the bag, and place the sealed bag in a bowl. Put the bowl in the refrigerator to marinate for 1-2 hours, shaking/turning the bag every 20-30 minutes. When the apples are finished marinating, remove them from the refrigerator.

4. Preheat the grill to medium-high heat. Grease the grill grates with high-heat cooking spray.

5. Transfer the marinated apple slices from the bag of marinade directly onto the grill grates (reserve the bag of marinade) and grill the apple slices for 3 minutes on each side, turning and basting with remaining marinade frequently.

6. Place 4 grilled apple slices onto each serving dish and drizzle the slices with any remaining marinade. Serve right away.

BARBECUE SAUCE RECIPES

Smoked Cherry Barbecue Sauce

A smooth, smoked cherry flavored barbecue sauce that is flavored with garlic, onion, maple syrup, among others. This sauce is delicious when used on grilled pork or lamb chops.

Yield: 3 cups
Servings: 12 (Serving Size: ¼ c.)
Total Time – Prep to Finish: 50 minutes

Ingredients:

- 2 tbsp. coconut oil
- 1 large yellow onion, chopped
- 6 cloves garlic, grated or pressed
- 3 c. cherries, pitted and smoked
- ¼ c. maple syrup
- ¼ c. apple cider vinegar
- 1 tsp. sea salt

Directions:

1. Place a cast iron skillet over medium heat. Add in coconut oil and allow it to heat up. Add in the onion and sauté for 7-10 minutes or until nicely browned and tender. Add in the garlic and sauté for 2 minutes or until fragrant.

2. Add in the smoked, pitted cherries, maple syrup, vinegar, and sea salt. Stir until well combined, then cook, uncovered for 20-30 minutes or until the mixture has thickened somewhat.

3. Transfer mixture to a blender and process until smooth.

4. Use immediately or pour into airtight mason jars for storage. Let the sauce cool completely at room temperature before placing the jars in the refrigerator for storage. Remains fresh in the refrigerator for up to 4 weeks.

Memphis-Style Barbecue Sauce

Memphis, Tennessee – home of Graceland, Beale Street, River Boats, and – of course – BBQ. BBQ which they are famous for. They are famous for their dry rubs and their barbecue sauces which carry a very distinctive flavor – a flavor, that when you taste it, you'll know that it's Memphis born. Well, now you can have that famous sauce anytime, in the comfort of your own home – and you don't have to go to Memphis to get it!

Yield: 3 cups
Servings: 12 (Serving Size: ¼ c.)
Total Time – Prep to Finish: 30 minutes

Ingredients:

- 2 tbsp. unsalted grass-fed butter (or ghee)
- 1 small onion, finely chopped
- 2 cloves garlic, minced
- 2 c. tomato sauce
- ½ c. apple cider vinegar
- 1/3 c. rice vinegar
- 1/3 c. molasses
- 3 tbsp. Worcestershire sauce
- 1 tbsp. maple syrup
- 1 tbsp. coconut palm sugar
- 2 tsp. yellow mustard
- 1 tsp. hot sauce
- 1 tsp. Kosher salt, or to taste
- 1 tsp. fresh ground black pepper, or to taste
- ¼ tsp. cayenne pepper

Directions:

1. Place a medium-sized pot over medium heat. Add in the butter and allow it to melt. Add in the onion; sauté for 5 minutes or until golden and fork tender. Add in the garlic and sauté for about 30 seconds or until fragrant.

2. Add tomato sauce, cider vinegar, rice vinegar, molasses, Worcestershire sauce, maple syrup, coconut palm sugar, mustard, hot sauce, salt, black pepper, and cayenne and stir to combine. Bring contents to a boil, then reduce heat to low and let simmer for 15-20 minutes, stirring occasionally, until the sauce has thickened slightly.

3. Transfer mixture to a blender and process until smooth.

4. Use immediately or pour into airtight mason jars for storage. Let the sauce cool completely at room temperature before placing the jars in the refrigerator for storage. Remains fresh in the refrigerator for up to 4 weeks.

Honey Barbecue Sauce

Here is a barbecue sauce that the whole family will love. A little sweet, a little spicy, a lot of possibility. This sauce literally tastes good with everything! Use as a sauce for grilling steak, use as a dip for chicken nuggets, or use for anything were a versatile sauce is needed. Quick and easy to make and stores well.

Yield: 2½ cups
Servings: 10 (Serving Size: ¼ c.)
Total Time – Prep to Finish: 20 minutes

Ingredients:

- 1 can (8 oz.) tomato sauce
- 2 tbsp. maple syrup
- 2 tbsp. honey
- 1 tbsp. fresh-squeezed lemon juice
- 1 tbsp. molasses
- 1½ tsp. Worcestershire sauce
- 1½ tsp. yellow mustard
- 1 garlic clove, minced
- ¼ tsp. dried oregano
- ¼ tsp. chili powder
- 1/8 tsp. fresh ground black pepper
- 1-2 tsp. hot sauce (opt. for heat)

Directions:

1. Place a medium-sized pot over medium heat. Stir in all of the ingredients in the order listed. Stir until thoroughly blended. Bring contents to a boil, then reduce heat to medium-low and let simmer for 10-15 minutes or until slightly thickened.

2. Use immediately or pour into airtight mason jars for storage. Let the sauce cool completely at room temperature before placing the jars in the refrigerator for storage. Remains fresh in the refrigerator for up to 4 weeks.

Mustard Barbecue Sauce

Here is a tangy BBQ sauce that is excellent on anything from salmon to steak to chops to ribs to ham and everything in between. It coats meat very well and is a grill aficionado's secret weapon.

Yield: 2½ cups
Servings: 10 (Serving Size: ¼ c.)
Total Time – Prep to Finish: 25 minutes

Ingredients:

- 1 c. chicken or beef broth
- 1 c. yellow mustard
- ½ c. red wine vinegar
- ¼ c. maple syrup
- ¼ c. coconut palm sugar
- 3 tbsp. grass-fed or coconut butter (or coconut oil)
- 2 tbsp. Worcestershire sauce
- 2 tbsp. tomato paste
- 2 tbsp. molasses
- 1 tbsp. garlic powder
- 1 tbsp. onion powder
- 1½ tsp. cayenne pepper
- 1 tsp. salt, or to taste
- ¼ tsp. fresh ground black pepper, or to taste

Directions:

1. Place a medium-sized pot over medium heat. Stir in all of the ingredients in the order listed. Stir until thoroughly blended. Bring contents to a boil, then reduce heat to medium-low and let simmer for 15-20 minutes or until slightly thickened. Remove from heat.

2. Use immediately or pour into airtight mason jars for storage. Let the sauce cool completely at room temperature before placing the jars in the refrigerator for storage. Remains fresh in the refrigerator for up to 4 weeks.

Honey-Pecan Barbecue Sauce

Here is a sweet, nutty-flavored BBQ sauce that goes well with any cut of beef, chicken, lamb, pork, or turkey. It is subtly sweet, a little spicy, extremely flavorful, and amazingly simple to prepare.

Yield: 3 cups
Servings: 12 (Serving Size: ¼ c.)
Total Time – Prep to Finish: 45 minutes

Ingredients:

- 1 can (12 oz.) tomato paste
- 1 c. pecans, ground
- ¾ c. water
- ¼ - 1/3 c. maple syrup (amount depending on preferred sweetness)
- 2 tbsp. coconut palm sugar
- ¼ c. apple cider vinegar
- ¼ c. onion, chopped fine
- ¼ c. honey
- 2 tbsp. fresh-squeezed lemon juice
- 1 tbsp. yellow mustard
- 2 garlic cloves, minced
- 1 tsp. Kosher salt, or to taste
- Pinch of fresh ground black pepper, or to taste.

Directions:

1. Put the pecans in a food processor and pulse until ground.
2. Place a medium-sized pot over medium heat. Add in the tomato paste, ground pecans, water, maple syrup, coconut palm sugar, vinegar, chopped onion, honey, lemon juice, yellow mustard, minced garlic, and salt. Stir until well blended. Bring contents to a boil, then reduce heat to medium-low and let simmer, stirring occasionally, for 15-20 minutes or until thickened slightly.
3. Transfer mixture to a blender and process until smooth.
4. Use immediately or pour into airtight mason jars for storage. Let the sauce cool completely at room temperature before placing the jars in the refrigerator for storage. Remains fresh in the refrigerator for up to 4 weeks.

34235013R00069

Made in the USA
Lexington, KY
02 August 2014